A Place at the Table

Participating in Community Building

Kathleen de la Peña McCook

WITH FOREWORD BY
Sarah Ann Long

AMERICAN LIBRARY ASSOCIATION
Chicago and London
2000

Design by Dianne M. Rooney

Composition by ALA Editions using ITC Fenice and Sabon typefaces

Printed on 50-pound white offset, a pH-neutral stock, and bound in 10-point cover stock by McNaughton & Gunn

The paper used in this publication meets the minimum requirements of American National Standard for Information Sciences—Permanence of Paper for Printed Library Materials, ANSI Z39.48-1992. ∞

Library of Congress Cataloging-in-Publication Data

McCook, Kathleen de la Peña.
    A place at the table : participating in community building / Kathleen de la Peña McCook.
        p.   cm.
    ISBN 0-8389-0788-1 (alk. paper)
    1. Libraries and society—United States. 2. Libraries and community—United States. 3. Community development—United States. 4. Library outreach programs—United States. 5. Coalition (Social sciences)   I. Title.

Z716.4 .M39 2000
021.2—dc21   00-038050

Printed in the United States of America.

04   03   02   01   5   4   3   2

To

Bill McCook

President,
Ruskin Civic Association,
1997–1999

Member,
United Brotherhood
of Carpenters,
for 37 years

CONTENTS

FOREWORD

I chose the theme "Libraries Build Community" for my year as ALA president because it is a fact (many libraries are involved in community building) and because I want to encourage libraries to step up their community building efforts. I also chose it as a way to get the message out to communities about the centrality of their libraries. The community idea applies to libraries of all types—academic, public, school, and special. No matter where you find a library, it is (or should be) the heart of the community it serves. Very often it is at the physical center of the community, and, as the information age develops, libraries as information nerve centers can serve both as access points and as interpretive points.

"Libraries Build Community" means collaborating and forming partnerships and alliances. To be effective, we need to work with other libraries, groups, organizations, and individuals who share our goals. Many libraries of all types already are involved in these kinds of partnerships, but I want to motivate libraries to move beyond the traditional partnerships and find the organizations that will help make the library a highly visible and integral part of the community. This is the overriding image that I want to project.

We all want to connect, to be in relationships with others. In these days of telecommuting and hopelessly tangled traffic, the local community is the one we long for, the one we relate to. People know about, pay attention to, and care about what's happening in their own backyards. This is not an original idea. All kinds of organizations have realized there's a community movement and are capitalizing on it. Hospitals talk about the Healthy Community Movement, and the newspaper industry is abuzz about Civic Journalism. At the same time, the Internet has created the potential for a new notion of community: the community of interest. People can find each other and get together electronically around an interest, a hobby, or a concern on the Internet. Geography (including distance, time zones, and traffic jams) doesn't matter.

As I have traveled around the country during my presidential year, I have been collecting stories about libraries that are community builders. You can find these stories on my Web site, *www.sarahlong.org*, but I wanted to mention one here because it is such a good example of my theme. Phyllis Cettomai and the Reed Memorial Library in Ravenna, Ohio, have been heavily involved in the Ravenna Bicentennial Commission, which planned a year's worth of events to celebrate the two hundredth anniversary of the city's founding.

The library is hosting the bicentennial calendar on its Web site and then adding pictures from the events. Staff members are in the process of adding a digital history project to their site. Reed Memorial is in the midst of a building project and Phyllis did not think she had time to get very involved in the bicentennial. The commission asked if the bicentennial quilt could be displayed in the library so Phyllis went to one meeting to talk about that and has never stopped. The library is presenting a monthly series of local history programs during the year. Staff members are using the library's local history collection to help add historic Ravenna citizens to the high school's hall of fame and then will digitize the material for the library's Web site. A member of the Reed board was instrumental in bringing an exhibit of the Ravenna, Italy, mosaics to town for their first display outside Europe as part of the yearlong celebrations, and there is information about that exhibit on the library's Web site.

Phyllis admits that although she is pretty tired, some very concrete benefits have come from the library's community involvement. The library has received incredible publicity and become highly visible in the community. The city now has a link from its Web site to the library's site and has added the library to its list of reasons for moving to Ravenna.

Two local history collections have been offered to the library—one from the local newspaper and the other from a private collector. Phyllis believes that all the favorable publicity will be a positive factor when residents are asked to vote for the library's building project.

Librarians have always talked at length about their libraries and they called that *lobbying*. Although it is important to talk about the library, if we really want to have effective partnerships and make a difference in our communities, we have to be part of the decision-making process in those communities. We have to be at the table with other organizations and government agencies. We have to be involved in giving and getting assets for the common good of the community.

When I was considering what theme I would choose, it wasn't too difficult for me to settle on something about libraries and community, but I struggled a bit with the words. For a long time it was going to be "The Library Is the Heart of the Community," but I decided that was not active enough. I really liked the idea of building. I hope you will focus on that active word *build,* and think about what you can do to make your library the heart of the community you serve. What activities can you undertake that will build the community as a constituency for your library? Who are your potential partners? With whom can you form an alliance? Who shares your goals? I hope that this book will inspire you to build links, partnerships, and connections for your library for the new millennium.

SARAH ANN LONG
ALA President
1999–2000

ACKNOWLEDGMENTS

I would like to extend my appreciation to Sara M. Taffae, Coordinator, Computer Services, State Library of Louisiana, for technical assistance; Gary O. Rolstad, Associate State Librarian, State Library of Louisiana, for his example of community building at a state level; Dean Bert R. Boyce, Louisiana State University, School of Library and Information Science, for inviting me as speaker at the December 1999 diploma ceremony at the school to see how these ideas would be received by new librarians; Kate Lippincott, Systems Librarian at the University of South Florida, Jane Bancroft Cook Library; the interlibrary loan departments of the University of South Florida Tampa Campus Library and the Tampa–Hillsborough County Public Library System; Dr. Derrie R. Perez, Interim Director, University of South Florida, Tampa Campus Library, for exploring these ideas; Marlene R. Chamberlain, Senior Editor, and Mary Huchting, Managing Editor, ALA Editions; and, most especially, Catherine Jasper, Arts and Letters Librarian, Tampa–Hillsborough County Public Library System, for reference assistance, electronic support, and manuscript preparation.

Sarah Ann Long, President, American Library Association, 1999–2000, deserves special appreciation for her theme "Libraries Build Community," and for requesting that I explore issues of community building for the association.

The Sense
of Community

Our nation longs for a sense of community. The ageographical nature of much of the landscape of places where people live in the United States has provoked discussion and proposals to find ways to build community.[1] Librarians have been part of this discussion, but they have not always been a part of the proposals. It is ironic that although librarians seem to understand very well their centrality to the delivery of a vital public service, and although citizens will laud the library in public venues, libraries are seldom mentioned or discussed in the broad literature of community building.

The status of libraries in the ongoing national dialogue on community is somewhat analogous to that of public schools—often perceived as a closed system because of inherent organizational structures. Yet libraries have been spectacularly successful in reconfiguring services in a period of rapid technological growth and, at the same time, maintaining great credibility in providing for community space.

The focus of this book is to discuss how to yoke the work of libraries in community building to the national movement to build community. Libraries are largely missing from the visioning statements about community, plans of community development foundations, designs by new urbanists, or writings on sustainability. By reviewing these movements and illustrating how libraries do, in fact, provide solutions to challenges of the crisis of place, it can be demonstrated that a librarian at every table is the solution that will lead to the inclusion of the work of librarians by the theorists and writers who seek to build community.[2]

Chapter 1 reviews the many dimensions of community, including issues surrounding enterprise and empowerment zones, suburbs, edge cities, and "fortress America." The chapter also summarizes the movement for civic renewal.

The second chapter discusses the recognition that diversity is a vigorous hope for a new society and identifies the strains on community building created by income disparity and a growing inequity between rich and poor. A reexamination of the role of the library in community development and restoration will identify the importance of the library as a natural locus for activation of the central needs of communities in social, cultural, and political spheres. Again, given the extensive efforts of librarians to develop multicultural collections, celebrate diverse cultures, and provide programming, it is disquieting to review books on the need to create more heterogeneous acceptance and find so little mention of the roles that libraries play.

Tying current library planning initiatives to community visioning initiatives is the focus of chapter 3. *Planning for Results* is used to demonstrate points of articulation with local and regional visioning and planning exercises.[3] The goal of the chapter is to describe the very strong intellectual and philosophical basis that libraries have forged to meet the needs of various communities. However, weak linkage at the initiating stages of larger visioning or with the work of such groups as community development foundations undercuts success at integration.

Factors for successful community building are presented in chapter 4. Although partnerships are a manifestation of two or more well-developed entities creating opportunities for collaboration that demonstrate shared goals and projects, they also tend to represent collaboration at the level of administrator to administrator. The chapter delineates how the work of librarians fits into a framework created by community building theorists. It is important to recognize that many of the components for community involvement are present in the work done by most public libraries. Librarians operate within a framing philosophy that should allow them to be active participants in community building.

Examples of community building by librarians are presented in chapter 5. Community building organizations suggested libraries they perceived as active in community building as they conceptualized it. This is important, for as much as the library profession is likely to characterize its work as contributory to community building, the external community building organizations seldom recognize this.

Cybercommunity building is discussed in chapter 6. The chapter explores key concepts that define the development of virtual communities and the librarian's roles in that development. In addition, chapter 6 identifies the existence of cybercommunity building outside libraries and describes ideological discomfort with the concept.

Chapter 7 connects examples of the work librarians do with comprehensive community building initiatives (CCIs). Using programmatic areas drawn from the CCI literature, "library responses" as listed in *Planning for Results* are suggested for each programmatic area.[4]

New models of work are necessary to realize the promise of true community building. Librarians who are part of their community activate the libraries that build community. This is the subject of chapter 8. Nothing short of revisiting each and every job description is needed with a focus on community development and revitalization. Ideas for this reemphasis are best defined in efforts to address the large systems that shape community life. Also described is the commitment that must be made by library administrators and leaders who affect policy. It is not enough that these complex concerns are left only to administrators who bring back ideas to already overcommitted staff. The frontline staff of libraries must be freed to engage in issues as they develop. Librarians cannot develop communities with eleventh-hour commitment.

The final chapter—really an envoi—is a reminder that we lose power when action ceases. By joining our past traditions to future opportunities with a sustained dedication to service, librarians will be valued as equal partners in community building enterprises.

There is little doubt that librarians who work in U.S. libraries have the ability, the sense of belief in human potential, and the resources to be vital to community building. Like a giant jigsaw puzzle, the pieces just need to be put in place. If activated through enhanced understanding as laid out in this volume, the restructuring of work to enable participation, and the incorporation of community building as a central library value, every single book and article about community building would include libraries and librarians as vital components.

The challenge is to have a librarian at every table.

ENDNOTES

1. Michael Sorkin, *Variations on a Theme Park: The New American City and the End of Public Space* (New York: Hill and Wang, 1992).

2. Timothy Beatley and Kristy Manning, *The Ecology of Place: Planning for Environment, Economy, and Community* (Washington, D.C.: Island Press, 1997).

3. Ethel Himmel and William James Wilson, *Planning for Results: A Public Library Transformation Process* (Chicago: American Library Association, 1998).

4. Ibid.

CHAPTER

1

The Many Dimensions of Community

"Libraries build community," the theme of millennium president of the American Library Association, Sarah Ann Long (1999–2000), reverberates for those who provide the public with library services.[1] This theme has great inclusiveness and appeals to the commitment of the profession to information equity and lifelong learning.[2] These ideals are included in the mission and value statements of libraries throughout the United States.

Committed as the profession is to this concept, however, the substantial literature about community building seldom mentions libraries. It is as if librarians operate in a parallel universe apart from community development groups, planners, or government agencies. The purpose of this chapter is to describe recent discussion on community to provide librarians who believe that we are fundamental to community building with the context needed to take the next step—the step that places librarians and library service as essential to community.

Definitions of *Community*, Its Perceived Decline, and the Need for Civil Society

If this exploration of how librarians can build community is to provide workable suggestions, there must first be an understanding of the term *community*. In libraries we speak of community quite broadly to indicate all whom we are mandated to serve. Where once this meant fairly precise taxing districts, libraries have, through interlocal agreements, reciprocal borrowing, interlibrary loan, and cyber access, extended our service bases. Thus, to librarians, "building community" might mean extension to people beyond governmental jurisdictions, but more often in the broader literature, the term seems to mean the geographic boundaries of taxed service or smaller neighborhood areas.

In the United States today, there is a great deal of discussion about the loss of a traditional sense of *place,* which is what most people conceptualize as "community." Cities have never been monolithic communities but, rather, many individual neighborhoods under a single government. As suburbs grew and as many became self-governing entities, each sought to establish itself as a special place endowed with characteristics manifested by a sense of a community of people who know each other and work together. However, as these suburbs flowed together with no real boundaries other than lines on maps, any sense of the suburbs as places with unique characteristics or special feelings of place has faded.[3] Small towns, perhaps the quintessential community in the golden patina of nostalgic visions, struggle with economic distress, as do the rural areas that sustain them.[4] Additionally, it is important to recognize that rural communities have economies based on a variety of activities, including agriculture, mining, and manufacturing, so few generalizations hold.[5]

In *The Spirit of Community,* his exposition of the communitarian philosophy, Amitai Etzioni observes that there are also nongeographic communities made of people who work together or share other social bonds.[6] He has clarified this expansive definition by stating that communities are groups of people who share affective bonds and cultures with a commitment to shared norms, values, and meanings.[7] Communities, then, may be shared territory, shared values, or even a sense of shared destiny.

Yet the ideal of community—be it geographic or social—has been seen by many as eroding in the face of declining civic engagement. This erosion has received broad attention lately, thanks to Robert D. Putnam.[8] Putnam's contention is that civic engagement has declined as measured by the number of citizens attending political meetings, serving on local organizations, committees, or working for political parties. Membership in and volunteering for civic organizations, such as parent-teacher associations, women's clubs, the League of Women Voters, the Red Cross, and the Girl and Boy Scouts, has fallen far below levels of the previous generation. At the same time, mass-membership organizations, such as the American Association of Retired Persons or the Sierra Club, have grown, and membership involvement simply means writing a check rather than creating an ongoing social bond.

What obstacles to community building exist in light of this decline in social capital? People feel they are too busy, suburbanization erodes a sense of connection, frequent moves make it difficult to feel a part of the neighborhood where one lives. The rise of chain stores, the decline of family businesses, and television as a replacement for group meetings have all contributed to a weakening of the sense of community. This disconnectedness is exacerbated by the growth of gated affluent communities that look within, rather than without, and disengage increasingly greater numbers of the professional classes from general civic involvement.[9] Gated communities share the definition of community as territory and are more inclined to be home owner associations (HOAs) rather than civic-based groups. "Residents view HOAs as a means of protecting their private property and guarding against intrusions. . . . [HOAs are] rooted in private property rights and ownership . . . not extending to the public shared community."[10]

These concerns have initiated an expanded debate and a call for new forms of civil society—"a rational response to social change—not a rebellion against the modern world but a new attempt to deal with modernity's discontents and dislocations. . . . an attempt to build the social, communal, ethnic, and neighborhood associations that suit these times."[11] Michael Walzer sees civil society as "the name of the space of uncoerced human association and also the set of relational networks— formed for the sake of family, faith, interest, and ideology—that fill this space."[12] In the civil society, people will be connected to each other and will feel responsible for each other.[13]

The focus on community in the 1990s—from the establishment of the communitarian movement in 1991, through the observations of Putnam on the decline of social capital, to the renewed call for a civil society—demonstrates that community as a concern has deeply engaged sociologists, political scientists, and philosophers at the level of values and beliefs.

Thus when we, as librarians, state that the libraries where we work "build community," we must realize that we are standing for a commitment to an evolving sense of communities and that, to build these communities, we must be fully informed about this evolution.

Initiatives to Build Community

Discussion of *community* is daunting because of the broad expansiveness of the term. As demonstrated earlier, there is concern that the spirit of community is diminishing even in affluent neighborhoods and small towns. To some degree, the focus on community in this nation over the past several decades has been on distressed communities in need of basic housing, services, and economic development. A brief summary of recent community building initiatives helps to clarify this discussion.

Nonprofit community development corporations (CDCs) promote stability in local communities through community revitalization. These organizations usually focus on a specific geographical area. Activities have centered on building houses, brokering financing, and revitalizing neighborhoods as multipurpose, community-controlled corporations.[14] A recent study by Alan C. Twelvetrees provides a brief history of the evolution of CDCs from poverty programs in the 1960s to local organizations striving to revitalize neighborhoods. In some cases, extant organizations, such as Chicago's Woodlawn Organization or Oakland's Spanish-Speaking Unity Council, became development organizations; in others, external support, such as the Bedford Stuyvesant Restoration Corporation (set up in Brooklyn by Senators Robert Kennedy and Jacob Javits) provided impetus.[15]

Today CDCs have taken a strong role in the social building of communities. Nationally, about two thousand CDCs are active, and their agendas include delivery of social services, economic development, community and resident organizing, and advocacy. It is difficult to characterize CDCs in general, however, as each is configured to meet the needs of a particular community. A recent study identifies general characteristics shared by most CDCs as they seek to build the social infrastructure. Areas of focus include leadership, security, employment, education, family skills and supports, health, public services, and community cohesion.[16] A number of resource agencies, usually foundation funded, have been established to provide support or funding for CDCs, including the Local Initiatives Support Corporation, which has as its purpose building neighborhoods with a true sense of community.[17] Another is the Center for Community Change, which increases the capacity of community-based organizations, connects people to resources, and provides on-site assistance to grassroots groups.[18]

The U.S. federal government has also taken action to build community through a joint initiative of the Department of Housing and Urban Development (HUD) and the U.S. Department of Agriculture (USDA). In 1994 President Bill Clinton designated 105 distressed communities as Empowerment Zones (EZs) and Enterprise Communities (ECs). In his National Urban Policy Report, then HUD Secretary Henry G. Cisneros stated that the Community Empowerment agenda would link families to work, leverage private investment, be locally driven, and affirm traditional values such as hard work, family, and self-reliance. This urban policy "is about building communities that work for people and America."[19] The companion policies for the rural United States are described in the mission statement of the USDA Office of Rural Development as creating self-sufficiency and long-term economic development to empower people and communities to work together to create jobs and opportunities.[20]

The variety of community building efforts supported by the EZs and ECs are identified in *What Works!*, a joint HUD/USDA publication outlining examples of how community-based partnerships in EZs and ECs have developed local solutions to problems.[21] The programs are overseen by the Community Empowerment Board chaired by (at the time) Vice President Al Gore and comprising heads of more than twenty cabinet agencies and executive offices intended to help cut through bureaucratic procedures on behalf of the EZ/EC communities. A midpoint analysis of these includes discussion of the difficulty in maintaining grassroots involvement once the bureaucratic structures retake control.[22]

The reports and studies that examine the activities of CDCs and Clinton's empowerment agenda fuel the broad focus on community building that filled the journals and conference programs of the 1990s. These real-world examples of community building as framed by general philosophical discussions begin to show us that the goal of libraries building community is appropriate and timely. However, library efforts have not been connected in ways that appear in the broad literature seeking to define community or in any of the discussions of CDCs, EZs, and ECs.

Community Building

Community building is difficult to define because, though the concept is long-standing, it changed and evolved with an increasing and broad-based national focus during the 1990s. A project to broaden the understanding of community building funded by the Annie E. Casey Foundation, the Rockefeller Foundation, and the U.S. Department of Housing and Urban Development resulted in the monograph *Community Building Coming of Age.*[23] This succinct review of the community building literature distills six thematic approaches and differentiates the "new" community building of the 1990s from the narrower neighborhood focus of the past. According to the monograph, community building is

> focused around specific improvement initiatives in a manner that reinforces values and builds social and human capital.
>
> community-driven with broad resident involvement.
>
> comprehensive, strategic, and entrepreneurial.
>
> asset-based.
>
> tailored to neighborhood scale and conditions.
>
> collaboratively linked to the broader society to strengthen community institutions and enhance outside opportunities for residents; consciously changing institutional barriers and racism.[24]

These six community building themes are central to success in the current milieu of social policy. According to the authors of *Community Building Coming of Age:*

> The feature that most starkly contrasts community building with approaches to poverty alleviation that have been typical in America over the past half-century is that its primary aim is not simply giving more money, services, or other material benefits to the poor. While most of its advocates recognize a continuing need for considerable assistance (public and private), community building's central theme is to obliterate feelings of dependency and to replace them with attitudes of self-reliance, self-confidence, and responsibility.[25]

Of course, by extension these themes apply to all communities, affluent or poor. Although the majority of the community building literature focuses on distressed communities, it is important to know how these discussions might be applied to all community situations. When more affluent communities are involved in community building, there is an increasing tendency for these activities to be characterized as civic involvement or civic renewal.

An effective catalyst for these concerns has been the Alliance for National Renewal, a coalition of more than two hundred national and local organizations dedicated to the principles of community renewal. Its motto is Unleashing the Power of Communities. The vision of the Alliance is for a renewed nation of communities that work for everyone.[26] The publications of the Alliance, notably *The Community Visioning and Strategic Handbook,* provide a map for the renewal of community.[27] The Alliance is a National Civic League program, and the League's motto is A Century of Community Building. The Alliance and the League have established a Community Assistance Team, which works with communities to provide technical assistance in various aspects of community building, including planning and visioning.

Community visions should reflect a community's common values. Development of a community vision is the process of bringing together all sectors of a community to identify problems, evaluate changing conditions, and build collective approaches to improve the quality of life in a community. Shared problem solving and planning for the future boost the community's collective self-esteem and pride and cause citizens to be invested stakeholders in their community's future.[28]

With technical assistance from the Alliance's Community Assistance Team, many communities have developed visioning statements as well as full-blown strategic plans. Communities with such plans include Fargo–Moorhead (Fargo, North Dakota, and Moorhead, Minnesota); St. Louis, Missouri; Blue Springs, Missouri; Scranton, Pennsylvania; Linn County, Iowa; Sioux Falls, South Dakota; and Indianapolis, Indiana. Many of these plans are available on the World Wide Web for review.

Each plan was formulated by interested community participants— some stakeholders by position or occupation (business owners, social services providers) as well as engaged citizens. Focus groups, task forces, and committees worked on different aspects of planning and visioning. Implementation might be through a CDC, a newly formed collaborative supported with a combination of local and foundation funds, or an ongoing core of citizens with shared vision. Some communities had external funding to produce their plan or vision; some relied on volunteers. A review of many of these plans reveals that these efforts provide a basis for community building as much through the process of discussion as through the achievement of a final product.

Community building, then, can be a focused effort to create a plan or vision for a broad community. It can be a process that is required to apply for EZ/EC funds, and implicit is the internalization of community building tenets. But community building can also take place within the context of lifelong learning and civic renewal.

Civic Renewal as Community Building

Parallel to the community building initiatives and growing from observations on the decline in civic engagement have been efforts to reinvigorate citizens of the United States with a sense of civic commitment—a new citizenship. This citizenship is the capacity developed by real-world public work that creates both a stake and standing in society through contribution.

The New Citizenship Project, at the Center for Democracy and Citizenship of the Humphrey Institute of Public Affairs, developed a white paper on "The New Citizenship" in 1993. It called for a partnership between citizens and government based on active citizenship as the foundation of politics, conceived as public problem solving. Such a partnership creates an enlarged perspective in which the individual's sphere of concern becomes transnational.[29]

In December 1994, a "Civic Declaration: Call for a New Citizenship" urged citizens to reclaim responsibility for and power over the nation's public affairs. It was set forth from "the vantage point of a 'third sector'—that vibrant array of voluntary associations, religious congregations, schools and colleges, the free press, professional groups, and community organizations that mediate between government and the market and that span the space between private life and mega-institutions."[30] The declaration identified a new generation of innovative leadership—citizen politicians—interested in engaging citizens more actively in government and public policy. There is a recognition that all communities have immense civic potential.

Ideas from the Civic Declaration and the Center for Democracy and Citizenship White Paper were discussed at Camp David before President Clinton's 1995 state of the union address to help the president think through civility and citizenship, the role of government in America, and the future of the American state in the information age.

These concepts were further clarified through the founding of the Alliance for National Renewal and the American Civic Forum. These groups have fostered the Civic Practices Network (CPN) as a learning collaborative for civic renewal.[31] The CPN is committed to revitalizing democracy to tackle the complex problems of the twenty-first century. Among more than fifty organizations affiliated with the CPN are the Center for Civic Networking, the Center for the Study of Community, the Communitarian Network, the Institute for the Study of Civic Values, Libraries for the Future, the National Civic League, the Pew Center for Civic Journalism, and Study Circles Resource Center. Activities of the organizations in this collaborative include working to develop civic skills at every level, empowering families, and developing community capacity for problem solving. Through the CPN, the work of these organizations is shared and dialogue encouraged.

An especially compelling worldview on civic renewal may be found in the publications of the Center for Living Democracy. The mission of the Center is to inspire and prepare people to make democracy a rewarding, practical, everyday approach to solving society's problems.[32] The vision of the center accommodates quite well the role of libraries in building community.

2000 and Beyond

Community, community building, civic renewal, and the ideal of a living democracy all characterize a dense philosophical and social justice theme in the last decade of the millennium in contrast with the far more visible coverage of the booming economy. Ironically, for the most part, libraries and librarians in the United States have been drawn away from these philosophical and sociological discussions as they have grappled with the concurrent surge of technological change. During the same period that a call for civic renewal resounded, librarians were assimilating the application of new technologies made possible by widespread adoption of the Internet and the World Wide Web. Thus it is highly appropriate that the American Library Association move into 2000 with a reassessment of what it means that libraries build community.

That we have done this there is no doubt; that others know we have done this and include us in their deliberations is far less certain.

Librarians have not been at the table during the national discussions about community building and the new citizenship. Librarians have not been prominent in the grants for EZs and ECs or in CDC planning. There has been little mention of libraries in visioning documents or plans by "new urbanist" designers. Libraries, like schools, are generally viewed as community services that are passive participants rather than proactive partners in broad visioning initiatives. Exceptions exist, but they have not been so visible as to move the work of librarians to a central role as documented in the national discussion of community building.

ENDNOTES

1. Sarah Ann Long, "Building Communities Is Our Business," *American Libraries* 30 (August 1999): 39.
2. Kathleen de la Peña McCook, "Using Ockham's Razor: Cutting to the Center. Prepared for the Professional Concerns Committee of the Congress on Professional Education." American Library Association, March 1, 1999. Accessed January 3, 2000. Available <*http://www.ala.org/congress/mccook.html*>.
3. Peter Newman, "Greening the City," in *Eco-City Dimensions,* ed. Mark Roseland (Gabriola Island, B.C.: New Society Publishers, 1997), 15.
4. Richard V. Francavilgia, *Main Street Revisited: Time, Space, and Image Building in Small-Town America* (Iowa City: University of Iowa Press, 1996).
5. Norman Walzer and Steven Deller, "Rural Issues and Trends: The Role of Strategic Visioning Programs," in *Community Strategic Visioning Programs,* ed. Norman Walzer (Westport, Conn.: Praeger, 1996), 5–6.
6. Amitai Etzioni, *The Spirit of Community* (New York: Crown, 1993), 121–122.
7. Amitai Etzioni, "The Attack on Community," *Society* 32 (July/August 1995): 12–17.
8. Robert D. Putnam, "Bowling Alone: America's Declining Social Capital," *Journal of Democracy* 6 (1995): 65–78; and "Tuning In, Tuning Out: The Strange Disappearance of Social Capital in America," *P.S. Political Science and Politics* 28 (1995): 664–683.
9. Edward J. Blakely and Mary Gail Snyder, *Fortress America: Gated Communities in the United States* (Washington, D.C.: Brookings Institution Press, 1997).

10. Ibid., 35.

11. E. J. Dionne Jr., "Introduction: Why Civil Society? Why Now?" in his *Community Works: The Revival of Civil Society in America* (Washington, D.C.: Brookings Institution Press, 1998), 7–8.

12. Michael Walzer, "The Idea of Civil Society: A Path to Social Reconstruction," in *Community Strategic Visioning Programs,* 123–124.

13. Ibid., 143.

14. Ford Foundation, *Seizing Opportunities: The Role of CDCs in Urban Economic Development* (New York: Ford Foundation, 1998).

15. Alan C. Twelvetrees, *Organizing for Community Development,* 2d ed. (Aldershot, Hants, England: Avebury, 1996), 7.

16. Mindy Leiterman and Joseph Stillman, *Building Community* (New York: Local Initiatives Support Corporation, 1993).

17. Local Initiatives Support Corporation, home page. Accessed November 8, 1999. Available *<http://www.liscnet.org>*.

18. Center for Community Change, home page. Accessed November 8, 1999. Available *<http://www.communitychange.org>*.

19. U.S. Department of Housing and Urban Development, Office of Policy Development and Research, *Empowerment: A New Covenant with America's Communities* (Washington, D.C.: HUD, 1995).

20. U.S. Department of Agriculture, *Strategic Plan of the USDA,* September 1997, section 8-5. Accessed November 8, 1999. Available *<http//www. usda.gov/ocfo/strat/index.htm>*.

21. *What Works! In the Empowerment Zones and Enterprise Communities,* vol. 2 (Washington, D.C.: HUD; USDA, 1997).

22. "EZ/ECs," *The Neighborhood Works* 20 (January–February 1997), entire issue.

23. G. Thomas Kingsley, Joseph B. McNeely, and James O. Gibson, *Community Building Coming of Age* (Washington, D.C.: The Development Training Institute; The Urban Institute, 1997). Accessed November 10, 1999. Available *<http://www.urban.org/community/combuild.htm>*.

24. Ibid.

25. Ibid.

26. Alliance for National Renewal. Accessed November 11, 1999. Available *<http://www.ncl.anr.org>*.

27. Derek Okubo, *The Community Visioning and Strategic Handbook,* 2d ed. (Denver: National Civic League Press; Alliance for National Renewal, 1997).

28. Derek Okubo, "Community Vision and Pride," in *Community Building*. Accessed November 11, 1999. Available *<http://www.ncl.org/ncl/cat11>*.

29. Harry Boyte, Benjamin Barber, Dorothy Cotton, Hal Saunders, and Suzanne Morse, "The New Citizenship: White Paper. A Partnership between Citizens and Government." Accessed November 10, 1999. Available *<http://www.cpn.org/sections/affiliates/white_paper.html>*.

30. "Civic Declaration: Call for a New Citizenship." Accessed November 9, 1999. Available *<http://www.cpn.org/sections/new_citizenship/civic_declaration.html>*.

31. Civic Practices Network, home page. Accessed November 8, 1999. Available *<http://www.cpn.org>*.

32. *Doing Democracy: The Quarterly Newsletter of the Center for Living Democracy* 6 (fall 1999).

2 Diverse Communities

The Challenge to Community Building

Those working for diversity are sometimes akin to a roundtable of knights of woeful countenance with grand hopes continually clashing with complex realities. Assaults on affirmative action, the rise of reverse discrimination complaints, continuing homelessness, and the triumph of welfare-to-work proponents have combined to change the landscape of community building. Librarians have been an extraordinarily positive force in these difficult times, often providing the third place of communal openness where diversity has a chance to thrive.[1] In this chapter, issues relating to diversity and community building are reviewed. Providing equal opportunity and valuing differences among people contribute to success in building diverse communities. Equal opportunity, by necessity, had to come first, for laws that prevented people from full participation as citizens remained in place. Valuing differences among people as an accepted ethos may be more difficult to achieve. For people to participate in community efforts, it is important that they be perceived by others as equal and having a culture and heritage that are seen as equal, even though different. It is not enough for the affluent to include but then condescend to those less well off. It is not enough for the majority group to persistently urge the minority groups that they need to be more like the majority.

Legal Solutions

Only in the past half-century have legal barriers to full participation in U.S. citizenship been eliminated, and it has often been through the oversight of the Equal Employment Opportunity Commission (established in 1965) that new laws have been enforced.[2] Though barely a generation has passed in which people, regardless of gender or ethnicity, have had the right to compete in a fair and open marketplace, to live where they wish, to enroll at schools of their choice, and to select their occupation, it is a continuous battle to ensure that these rights remain open. Through affirmative action, women and people of color have been encouraged to expand their options and, at various times, have been given preference or extra support through scholarships for entry to schools or occupations in an effort to bring their participation in specific areas more in line with their numbers in the general population.

Recent actions in courts and at the ballot box, however, show that sympathy for affirmative action for those who historically have been shut out is waning:

> The *Hopwood* decision in Texas ended admission of college students based on ethnicity and affects not only Texas but, potentially, Mississippi and Louisiana (Fifth Circuit).[3]

> In California, Proposition 186 prevents illegal aliens from receiving benefits or public services, and Proposition 209 prevents California from giving preferential treatment based on race or gender in public education, employment, or contracting.

> In Florida, Executive Order 99-281 ended preferential hiring, state contracting, or admission to higher education based on race, gender, creed, or national origin.[4]

These are all indications that efforts to redress past discrimination are losing ground. Couched as "antidiscrimination," these new measures take U.S. society back to preaffirmative-action days. Though the language of these various initiatives provides for different approaches to achieve equality, the force of law is lifted.

The effect of these backlash measures is yet to be fully understood, although the first year of admissions to higher education in California under Proposition 209 (1998) showed a decline in the enrollment of African Americans and Latinos. Certainly this change in attitude toward the larger community of all populations will have some effect in communities at the grassroots level.

Valuing Difference

While the guarantees of fairness as legislated and adjudicated continue to evolve, there have been advances in valuing diversity that cut across all aspects of U.S. society. Today curricular guidelines for schools and universities identify attention to multicultural issues as an important aspect of education. Hard-won efforts to establish academic departments of African American Studies, Latino Studies, Asian American Studies, Native American Studies, Women's Studies, or Queer Studies were seen as necessary to enable multicultural scholars to have an academic role and students a way to understand the cultures and art of those outside the Euro-American mainstream. As these disciplinary programs have gained their place in the academy, students, presumably, now graduate with a far more diverse understanding of the world than did those of the preceding generation.

Additionally, immigrant children and U.S.-born children of immigrants number 13.4 million and make up 20 percent of all U.S. children. As they take part in U.S. society, the transformation of culture will be profound.[5]

The success of the civil rights movement in establishing equality for all people opened the door for the valuing of their cultures. Teachers added authors from non-European cultures for reading and discussion. Communities began to take note of special days and events of different cultures, such as Passover, Juneteenth, Cinco de Mayo, the Chinese Lunar Festival, Vaisakhi, or Ramadan. Appreciation for diverse cultures has been generally accepted as important to the United States in the beginning days of this century.

This has not come about with ease. Faculties have struggled to revise curricula; cities and towns have slowly recognized the need to expand civic celebration to be more inclusive of the traditions of other cultures; and the mass media have needed to be reminded again and again that the face of the United States is made of many colors. At first it was difficult to value difference; it was troublesome to write names with diacritics, hard to have an appreciation for music with a different rhythm, tiresome to go to yet another meeting to discuss inclusion.

Then, somewhere along the line, all this was not troublesome, hard, or tiresome—it was right and it expanded the worldview of those who made the effort.

Diversity of Economic Status and Place

Less discussed than diversity based on culture, but critical to understand if community building is to be successful, is diversity of economic status and place. Those who live in the United States like to think ours is a classless society, a meritocracy with upward mobility available to all. The economic prosperity in the last years of the 1990s provided a sense that all boats are rising. This perception is underscored by the decline in welfare rolls since the 1996 Welfare Reform Act (Work Opportunity Reconciliation Act) went into effect with its limits on the number of months a family can receive cash aid. The results are not yet in.

Even for those former welfare recipients now at work, this engagement in the workforce is a fragile participation that may erode when child care, health care, and transportation subsidies are reduced as wages improve.[6] Those at the bottom of the economic pyramid experience tremendous anxiety and are often just a paycheck away from collapse. Many who have gone off welfare are working at minimum wage and, even with the Earned Income Tax Credit, may need several jobs.

This situation persists. Income disparity is greater today than ever before. For the United States as a whole, the average family income of the top 20 percent ($137,500) was ten times as large as that of the poorest 20 percent ($13,000).[7] It is very difficult to involve people working long days at physically demanding jobs in community building.

There continues to be a large group of disenfranchised who, though perhaps never on welfare, are underemployed, unemployed, or homeless and coping in ways not visible. In *Cold New World: Growing Up in a Harder Country,* William Finnegan explores the fact that

> this country was (and is) in a strange, even an unprecedented, condition. While the national economy has been growing, the economic prospects of most Americans have been dimming. For young people and males and those without advanced degrees—for, that is, the large majority of working Americans—real hourly wages have fallen significantly over the past twenty-four years . . . leaving 30 percent of the country's workers earning too little to lift a family out of poverty.[8]

Homelessness also continues as a factor that must be considered in a review of economic issues. The 1999 Urban Institute report found the median income of the homeless was $367 a month—51 percent of the poverty level. The homeless are vulnerable in many ways—low levels of educational achievement, few job skills, lack of family, substance abuse, mental illness, and experience with incarceration.[9] The homeless are 49 percent African American, 32 percent Caucasian, 12 percent Hispanic, 4 percent Native American, and 3 percent Asian. Forty percent of the homeless are veterans. The homeless are rural and urban.[10]

Poverty, as defined by the U.S. government, shifts every year. The 1998 "poverty threshold" was $16,600 for a family of four.[11] Though the poverty rate (the percentage of the U.S. population whose annual income does not meet the poverty threshold) had declined to 12.7 percent as of 1998, the actual number of people in poverty had increased to 34.5 million.[12]

Indeed, the change in the nature of work has been another factor in the dismantling of community. The decline in the strength of labor unions, once an agency for working-class solidarity, has been caused by many factors, including deterritorialization as production moved to areas with cheaper labor costs. The result is that as work shifts, community and culture are separated from the labor process and no longer depend upon the socializing function of the workplace for their vitality.[13]

Education is viewed as the means by which the working class can participate in the general economic boom, but it is a misperception to think that this door has been opened to all. Seventeen percent of the U.S. population over age twenty-five have not completed high school. Adults over age twenty-five with four or more years of college accounted for only 23.9 percent of the overall U.S. population in 1997. The percentage of adults completing college varies by ethnicity, with Asian Americans/Pacific Islanders at 42.2 percent, whites at 24.6 percent, African Americans at 13.3 percent, and Hispanics overall at 10.3 percent (Hispanics of Cuban heritage, 19.7 percent; of Puerto Rican heritage, 10.7 percent; and of Mexican heritage, 7.5 percent).[14]

Given these numbers, it is important that community builders seek strategies to work across economic levels to find ways that people can come together. Too often when attempts are made to understand a community, the voices of the educated dominate because they have the time and the skills to participate. Rather than focus wholly on diversity by ethnicity, it is also vital to understand issues that result from economics.

Poor people are often excluded from discussions because they have less access to public discursive space. Their stories are told by others. In her analysis of autobiographies of working-class women, Roxanne Rimstead notes that their lives become more meaningful to readers through the specificities of history and place and foster a more receptive attitude to the psychological differences created by material distress and social exclusion.[15]

Rural communities experience a completely different degree of separation from the larger culture, and many who live in rural areas feel increasingly alienated. In a monograph that explores this alienation, Joel Dyer observes,

> As we plow ahead into the next millennium, a high-tech global market-place and an increasingly global monetary system are forcing working-class and farming rural peoples to compete on a rapidly leveling playing field with their Third World counterparts. This is a nasty proposition for someone born into the American dream, someone who already finds the standard of living harsh and unacceptable.[16]

Yet rural poverty continues to be difficult to understand, and studies tend more to point out questions than to offer answers. Rural poverty is seen as a paradox. Traditions of families who have lived in rural areas are comforting, but stifling; self-provisioning (the ability to enhance one's day-to-day living by growing food or through barter) is viable, but exhausting; kin networks both protect and smother; ties to the land are comforting, but constraining.[17]

Moving closer to population centers, the suburbs, and edge cities, other concerns about community arise. The edge city, characterized by Joel Garreau, (1) has five million or more square feet of leasable office space; (2) has 600,000 or more square feet of leasable retail space; (3) has more jobs than bedrooms; (4) is perceived by the population as one place; and (5) was nothing like a city thirty years ago. Examples are Schaumburg, Illinois; the Perimeter Center area at the northern tip of Atlanta, Georgia; Irvine, California; the Massachusetts Turnpike and Highway 128; and the Katy Freeway–West Houston Energy Center Corridor.[18]

In an excruciating effort to define community in edge cities by asking people in Orange County, California, for their definition, Garreau includes the Southern California Technology Executives, the South Coast Community Church, and Great Expectations (high-tech matchmaking)—voluntary communities rather than geographical. Garreau asked Tom Nielsen, the leading light for Irvine, California, billed as America's premier master-planned community, "What does community mean to you?" Nielsen answered, "It doesn't mean anything more than a marketing term."[19]

Suburbs present another set of concerns regarding community. Though much has been written since the era of the Levittowners, suburbs continue to be a topic of study and opinion.[20] In a discussion of the types of art produced by different communities, the suburbs are seen as a site of contradictions—lacking clear lines of kinship and providing instead an isolated subjectivity, a social autism of intrapersonal anxiety. In suburbs, productive forces are disguised in industrial parks and public space is the shopping mall. Labor is invisible; only consumption is visible.[21]

In an essay attempting to understand how Olathe, a suburb of Kansas City, had become an area of Christian conservatism, Peter Beinart notes that "the Christian right is not a rural movement, it is a suburban one."[22] He contends that the lack of organic community in the suburbs, with life revolving about shopping malls, and the lack of a civic life have made possible the extraordinary growth of evangelical churches. To an extent, evangelical churches are as much community centers as places of worship.

Affluence and poverty sit side by side in the United States. Nowhere is this as striking as in Los Angeles where there is no middle. High-paying jobs, especially in technology, accompany a "raging torrent of low-wage work that barely deserves the adjective *subsistence.*"[23]

The increase in gated community developments like Hidden Hills (with the highest per-capita income of any city in California) outside Los Angeles, which has incorporated as an independent city, is an indicator that differentiation by income level is another divisive factor in community building.[24] Writing of gated communities, Edward Blakely and Mary Gail Snyder observe,

Community is more than a set of local social relationships in America. . . . As place and community become commodified, environments we buy into rather than we create, our neighborhoods are more and more shaped by economic rather than social institutions. . . . Walls and gates are more than obstructions to entry; they are symbols of a new social pattern that may have profound effects on the nation itself.[25]

Robert D. Kaplan also explores these ideas in *An Empire Wilderness: Travels into America's Future,* in which he sees our nation developing into a highly segregated society of global marketplace winners in office parks and gated communities and service workers in rotting neighborhoods as he explores St. Louis, Tucson, Omaha, and Orange County.[26]

In fact, the growth of private community organizations nationwide may be an indicator that for many people, community is defined as private space over which they have a greater measure of control than they do over larger units of government. The growth of the Community Associations Institute (CAI), the lobbying association for community associations, condominium associations, and home owner associations and cooperatives that represents 205,000 entities, may indeed underscore what Robert B. Reich characterizes as the "secession of the successful."[27]

Ironically, those in gated communities want to build community, too. The CAI has just released a new book titled *Community First!* that offers techniques for fostering community spirit; establishing a mission statement and strategic plan; empowering associations to provide social, educational, wellness, and other services; and linking to the larger community.[28] The same theme emerges whether it is an inner-city neighborhood, a rural small town, an amorphous suburb near an edge city, or a gated community of million-dollar homes: Everybody wants community.

Unifying around Diversity

Community builders sometimes make assumptions about the way people want to live and impose certain value-laden goals in the process of developing community visions that may, in fact, drive away all but the like-minded. The most extreme version of this is in the communities with deed restrictions and covenants that enforce strict guidelines of community appearance down to the colors of window trim or whether to allow visitors who drive pickup trucks.

This chapter demonstrates that diversity of ethnicity and socioeconomic class and place make community building complex. There are many vantage points from which community can be viewed. Diversity expands rather than clarifies the task of community building. Nevertheless, without an attempt to explore the many aspects of diversity, those who seek to be community builders would need to address these issues anew. By presenting some sense of the breadth of what is meant by diversity for building community, we can go on to identify steps to take.

ENDNOTES

1. Terry Pindall, *A Good Place to Live: America's Last Great Migration* (New York: Holt, 1995).

2. *Brown v. Board of Education*, 1954; Civil Rights Act, 1964; Voting Rights Act, 1965; Age Discrimination Act of 1967; Americans with Disabilities Act of 1990.

3. J. Selingo, "University of Texas at Austin Ends Minority Hiring Program," *Chronicle of Higher Education* (January 15, 1999).

4. Florida, Executive Office of the Governor, Executive Order 99–281, November 9, 1999.

5. Rubén G. Rumbaut, "Transformations: The Post-Immigrant Generation in an Age of Diversity," JSRI Research Report no. 30 (East Lansing, Mich.: The Julian Samora Research Institute, Michigan State University, 1999).

6. Jack A. Meyer, "Assessing Welfare Reform: Work Pays," *Public Interest* 136 (summer 1999): 113–120.

7. Jared Bernstein et al., *Pulling Apart: State-by-State Analysis of Income Trends* (Washington, D.C.: Economic Policy Institute and Center on Budget and Policy Priorities, January 2000). See also Frank Levy, *The New Dollars and Dreams: American Incomes and Economic Change* (New York: Russell Sage, 1998).

8. William Finnegan, *Cold New World: Growing Up in a Harder Country* (New York: Random House, 1998), xiii.

9. Martha R. Burt et al., *Homelessness: Programs and the People They Serve: Summary Report: Findings of the National Survey of Homeless Assistance Providers and Clients* (Washington, D.C.: The Urban Institute, December 1999).

10. Scott Logan, *The Face of Homelessness* (Issue Brief: Critical Issues for County Officials) (Washington, D.C.: National Association of Counties, October 1999), 3.

11. U.S. Census Bureau, Current Population Survey. Accessed November 16, 1999. Available *<http://www.census.gov/hhes/poverty/threshld/thresh98.html>*.

12. U.S. Census Bureau, Current Population Survey, March 1969 to 1999. Accessed November 16, 1999. Available <*http://www.census.gov.hhes/www/img/incpov98/chart4.gif*>.

13. Stanley Aronowitz, *The Politics of Identity: Class, Culture, and Social Movements* (New York: Routledge, 1992), 246.

14. U.S. Bureau of the Census, Census of Population. Accessed November 16, 1999. Available <*http://www.census.gov/statab/freq/98s0260.txt*>.

15. Roxanne Rimstead, "Subverting Poor Me: Negative Constructions of Identity in Poor and Working-Class Women's Autobiographies," in *The Language and Politics of Exclusion: Others in Discourse,* ed. Stephen Harold Riggins (Thousand Oaks, Calif.: Sage, 1997), 262.

16. Joel Dyer, *Harvest of Rage* (Boulder, Colo.: Westview Press, 1997), 71.

17. Patricia Garrett and Naurine Lennox, "Rural Families and Children in Poverty," in *Persistent Poverty in Rural America,* Rural Sociological Society Task Force on Persistent Poverty (Boulder, Colo.: Westview Press, 1993), 235.

18. Joel Garreau, *Edge City: Life on the New Frontier* (New York: Anchor Books/Doubleday, 1991).

19. Ibid., 301.

20. Herbert Gans, *The Levittowners: Ways of Life and Politics in a New Suburban Community* (New York: Pantheon, 1967). See also M. P. Baumgartner, *The Moral Order of a Suburb* (New York: Oxford University Press, 1988).

21. Maureen P. Sherlock, "Moral Minimalism and the Suburban Spectacle,"*Art Papers* 22 (May/June 1998): 22–25.

22. Peter Beinart, "Battle for the 'burbs,'" *New Republic* 219 (October 19, 1998): 25–29.

23. Edward W. Soja, "Los Angeles, 1965–1992: From Crisis-Generated Restructuring to Restructuring-Generated Crisis," in *The City: Los Angeles and Urban Theory at the End of the Twentieth Century,* ed. Allen J. Scott and Edward W. Soja (Berkeley, Calif.: University of California Press, 1996), 446.

24. Andrew Stark, "America, the Gated?" *Wilson Quarterly* 22 (winter 1998): 58–79.

25. Edward J. Blakely and Mary Gail Snyder, *Fortress America: Gated Communities in the United States* (Washington, D.C.: Brookings Institution Press, 1997), 35.

26. Robert D. Kaplan, *An Empire Wilderness: Travels into America's Future* (New York: Random House, 1998).

27. Robert B. Reich, *The Work of Nations: Preparing Ourselves for 21st-Century Capitalism* (New York: Knopf, 1991).

28. Community Associations Institute, *Community First! Emerging Visions: Reshaping America's Condominium and Homeowner Associations* (Alexandria, Va.: CAI, 1999). See also Evan McKenzie, *Privatopia: Homeowner Associations and the Rise of Residential Private Government* (New Haven: Yale University Press, 1994).

3 Visions of Community

*Toward Comprehensiveness
and a Library Presence*

Public libraries are part of the larger community. Although it is a true that the vision, mission, and goals of the larger community by necessity guide the library in its own planning, it is a truth that requires analysis if librarians are to take their place as community builders. This book focuses on public libraries; therefore, the entire community that the library serves must be considered.[1]

In the two previous chapters, the complex and evolving definitions of community have been explored as well as various government, nonprofit, and social services strategies to enhance communities. The diverse nature of communities has been described to characterize the variety of people and settings that must be kept in mind.

A fresh look at community building is presented in *City Making: Building Communities without Building Walls*, by Gerald E. Frug.[2] Frug proposes a number of ways to increase the exercise of public freedom, argues for the development of more public space to increase metropolitan residents' comfort with and knowledge of their region's diversity, and proposes a new legal definition of cities designed to open city borders.[3] Because libraries provide a near-perfect embodiment of a city service that has the potential to further community building objectives, Frug's framework offers a different way to think about community building that at once values diversity and presents a realistic analysis of possibilities. The paradox, once more, is that of all the examples Frug offers, libraries are not among them. How do librarians become included in the roster of service that community theorists contemplate as they develop their models?

Envision: Imagining the Future

Planning for Results: A Public Library Transformation Process was developed as one of an ongoing series of planning publications produced by the Public Library Association. "It is intended to help public library directors, staff, and board members manage the future rather than . . . react to the present."[4] The third chapter, "Envision: Imagining the Future," presents a summary of the need to imagine the future through six planning tasks:

1. Articulate a community vision.
2. Scan the community.
3. Identify community needs.
4. Scan the library.
5. Determine which community needs the library should address.
6. Write the library vision statement.[5]

The first of these tasks, "articulate a community vision," gives a passing reference to community vision initiatives but does not provide any sense of the current sweeping national movement to develop community visions. If a library preparing to begin the planning process finds that no community vision has been developed, *Planning for Results* suggests that the library "act as a catalyst to get the community-wide process started."[6] This seemingly simple suggestion does not give users of the manual sufficient information to begin to explore the connections that must be made for a community visioning process to be successful. The subsequent description of planning tasks suggests that in lieu of a community statement, the library develop "a skeletal community vision statement of its own."[7] The decision to do so, however, might well place the library outside the community building framework and lock it into its own closed circle. Instead, librarians endeavoring to initiate or participate in visioning should be aware of the current national context for community planning and visioning.

Two overarching community building movements that have helped formulate national thinking during the past decade are sustainable development and organic planning. A brief look at each of these will provide an additional framework for understanding the scope of community building.

Sustainable Development

Sustainable development came to worldwide attention with the publication of *Our Common Future* in 1987. Often called the Brundtland Report, this global agenda for change is a mandate for development that will meet the needs of the present without compromising the ability of future generations to meet their own needs.[8] In 1992 the United Nations Commission on Sustainable Development was established to monitor implementation of the plan, forged by the UN Conference on Environment and Development, to achieve sustainable development in the twenty-first century.

Shortly after the establishment of the UN Commission, President Clinton created the President's Council on Sustainable Development (PCSD) with a mission to

> Forge consensus on policy by bringing together diverse interests to identify and develop innovative economic, environmental, and social policies and strategies;
>
> Demonstrate implementation of policy that fosters sustainable development by working with diverse interests to identify and demonstrate implementation of sustainable development;
>
> Get the word out about sustainable development; and
>
> Evaluate and report on progress by recommending national, community, and enterprise level frameworks for tracking sustainable development.[9]

The first phase of the PCSD resulted in several task force reports pertinent to community visioning. "Public Linkage, Dialogue, and Education," released in February 1997, included "Expanding Community Visioning" as Action Task 4. Here the visioning process is explained with examples of communities that have developed visions, such as Greenville County, South Carolina; Noblesville, Indiana; Owensboro, Kentucky; Plymouth, Wisconsin; Santa Ana Pueblo, New Mexico; and Seattle, Washington. Organized around the concept of sustainability, this task force makes it clear that without community involvement, visioning is ineffective.[10]

Another task force report of the PCSD titled *Sustainable Communities* is exuberant in its idealism. It states:

> Communities will expand opportunities and incentives for civic involvement, and they will recommit schools and other community institutions to civic education. They will encourage citizens to look beyond short-term self-interest to the long-term common interest. Widespread participation in programs to envision a sustainable future and to identify shared community goals will help restore a sense of common purpose. . . . These developments will affect the national psyche to the point where Americans feel a strong sense of community has renewed our capacity to work together to solve problems and improve our neighborhoods, communities, and ultimately, our lives.[11]

The entire Sustainable Communities initiative provides a rich foundation for thinking about community building. In the final report of the President's Council, *Towards a Sustainable America: Advancing Prosperity, Opportunity, and a Healthy Environment for the 21st Century*, the section on "Local Capacity and Partnerships: Creating 'Civic DNA'" describes the results of building local capacity:

> A comzmunity must be able to create its own vision of the future, develop and implement it in conjunction with the public and private sectors, and assess progress towards that vision. The capability is vested in an array of formal and informal networks of individuals and institutions. When a community is rich in this capability, there is a strong community spirit manifested in myriad ways: strong local philanthropy, volunteerism, workers commitment to business, and business support of community incentives. As much of the social and cultural landscape in the United States undergoes profound change, communities are challenged to re-create the webs of local interaction that nurture local capacity and community spirit.[12]

This national presidential initiative provides support to the efforts of the associations and groups described in the first chapter as they move toward a renewed focus on community.

The voluntary nature of many structures for participatory decision making in the United States without formal governmental authority can exert considerable influence in community development.[13] Understanding the sustainable development movement is important for articulating library vision with community vision. Although it is difficult to get a good grasp of the vast sweep of this international movement, it is necessary in understanding community building today.

Organic Planning

Planning appears to be an arena in which everybody has a different approach. The need to plan has been internalized by organizations, governments, and businesses. Sustainability informed many community visioning and planning initiatives in the 1990s. Yet reasons for the decision to plan can remain somewhat ambiguous.

An external requirement to do so—to apply for Enterprise Zone funds, for example—may be a reason to plan. A representative example of this type of planning can be viewed at the Web site for the Chicago, Illinois, Empowerment Zone describing the plan developed by the community. There it is noted that HUD requires a "bottom-up" strategic plan. The Strategic Neighborhood Action Program initiated by Chicago has been cited as a model of Empowerment Zone strategy in that it requires community input.[14]

Complicating the mix is the fact that many governments have planning departments and retain professional planners whose roles may include the creation of community or neighborhood plans. Philadelphia's City Planning Commission includes a division of "Community Planning" that lists as a responsibility "maintaining a citizen participation process."[15] Additionally, elected officials can initiate a planning process, as in the "Livable Tucson Vision Program" launched by the mayor and the council.[16]

With so much invested in planning and visioning by government entities, the suggestion that a library might act as a catalyst is somewhat heedless. This is not to say that librarians could not play this role, but, rather, that choosing to play this role would mean investing a great deal of work and time before the decision to do so. Flowing from citizen participation seen as optimal in the movement toward visioning for sustainable communities is an evolutionary approach called organic planning.

Organic planning is citizen-led, future-oriented planning aimed at improving local government and communities. It can exist independent of institutional sponsorship; it is more process oriented than end oriented; it offers a distinctive venue of deliberation that shapes issue consideration and policy alternative formulation. When citizen groups collaborate in addressing community issues that have been viewed as the domain of government entities, a new type of community vision can emerge. Visioning that is future oriented, inclusive, and focused on a tangible outcome of deliberation (a vision statement) may be characterized as organic, especially when it is rooted in community interaction rather than in fixed institutional or governmental players.[17]

Assaying the role of governments in the twenty-first century, Bryan T. Downes observes, "Realizing a sustainable future, a new vision, and initiating new decision making processes needed to deal with complex, interconnected, conflict provoking issues requires new leadership and corresponding culture change."[18] It is this vision and these decision-making structures that libraries seeking to "plan for results" must reach to and interconnect with in all areas of concern. Libraries will need to be sure they have considered the tenets of community participation and organic planning before launching independent vision projects. This is where knowing the community is crucial. Those who favor organic planning might see the library as yet another governmental entity seeking to catalyze a vision process for its own end.

Comprehensive Community Initiative

For librarians who want to build community, it is important to understand and monitor the community building movement as it evolves. Chapter 1 summarized the evolution of the concept through the 1990s, especially against the background of the movement for civic engagement and renewal. The process of improving the quality of life in a neighborhood by strengthening the capacity of neighborhood residents, associations, and organizations to identify priorities and opportunities and to work, individually and collectively, to foster and sustain positive neighborhood change is another working definition provided by the Roundtable on Comprehensive Community Initiatives for Children and Families of the Aspen Institute.[19]

Comprehensive community initiatives (CCIs) have the goal of promoting positive change and operate on the premise that the devolution of authority and responsibility from higher-level entities to the neighborhood or community is a necessary aspect of the change process. Rooted in earlier neighborhood efforts, including the community development corporation (CDC) movement, CCIs are based on the principles of comprehensiveness and community building. Their stronger emergence during the 1990s can be attributed to (1) recognition by human services professionals that fragmentation in service delivery was limiting program success; (2) realization that high costs in service domains called for more effective strategies; (3) recognition that the focus on housing rehabilitation, especially through the CDCs, was not achieving sustained improvement in low-income neighborhoods; and (4) increasing acceptance that, for both pragmatic and ideological reasons, public–private partnerships and local action are alternatives to big government.[20] CCIs work to build synergy across a neighborhood's physical, economic, and social sectors and to build community by strengthening the capacity of people, institutions, and associations for enhanced community well-being.

The CCI approach has grown because of increased awareness of the need for cross-sector, cross-system reform and the recognition that individual lives must be connected with the community to achieve real change. The CCI model has evolved along with the CDC model as a realization that comprehensive planning and implementation are more effective than categorical approaches to problem solving and community change. It is far more likely that librarians can be effective in the CCI model rather than the CDC model. As the community building model has shifted, however, there is less clarity for community planning as the development of organizational capacity is harder to measure.

Capacity, a term initially used to reflect the effect of CDCs on increasing housing, has been expanded to mean what is needed to achieve enough development to have an impact on all developmental aspects of a neighborhood.[21] To some extent the increase in the use of capacity as a measure of community strength emanates from its use in documents issued by the United Way of America. Because of its scope and influence, the United Way has been extraordinarily effective in shifting the manner in which social services agencies develop plans. It is a vast network of 1,400 independent organizations that raised $3.4 billion in 1997–1998 and supported 45,000 agencies.[22] Capacity building, in part because of the influence of the United Way construct, has come to mean the linkage of specific program outcomes with community outcomes. The struggle of the relationship between the two has made it clear to United Way policy makers that achieving community change requires more than funding. There must be a comprehensive strategy.[23]

The 1999 United Way of America White Paper on Change discusses how two tools—community status reports and targeted community interventions—relate in building stronger communities. The tasks of targeted community intervention include

> developing a comprehensive action strategy for achieving outcomes
>
> developing a detailed action plan describing how to implement the strategy: what, by whom, with whom, and when
>
> deciding what indicators/information will show the extent to which the outcomes and milestones are being achieved
>
> developing and implementing a plan for measuring outcome indicators[24]

Of all the organizations and coalitions working today to build community, the United Way—because of its scope and national penetration—must be taken into careful consideration. Community visioning and planning done without understanding the similar but perhaps more specific guidelines that agencies funded by the United Way must meet will run parallel and perhaps be counterproductive.

Community building has come to be a bellwether as the new century begins. Yet this concept, which seems easy to understand at first glance, is extraordinarily multifaceted. Adding to the complexity is the difference in expectation of the product-driven approaches (CDCs, United Way) compared with the process-driven (CCIs, EZs/ECs). And confounding the picture has been the movement for those initiatives with a strong product component to seek greater comprehensiveness.

The dynamics of these issues have been explored in an effort to suggest the steps that need to be taken to operationalize comprehensive community building. The tension between product and process plays out in several arenas:

> *Efficiency versus participation:* That is, building capacity or getting things done. Community revitalization depends on capacity building even at the expense of completing a list of objectives quickly. Without participation of community-level residents, there will be no transformation of the community.
>
> *Expertise versus facilitation:* Bringing in technical experts may be the fastest way to deliver a product to the community, but it fails to involve the community. Coaching community residents

when technical issues arise and facilitating their involvement in finding solutions builds capacity.

Concrete projects versus community building: Weaving community building activities into all aspects of a CCI's work can develop community leadership around problem solving. This will make even focus on very tangible projects one that will empower the residents.

Counting products versus assessing capacity: Evaluating the success of a CCI is far easier through the analysis of completed projects than through the assessment of community building progress. To counteract this tendency, evaluation mechanisms for the community building components need to be in place at the initiative's outset.

Additionally, and this is a factor to which any government-supported entity must be sensitive, there is an "inside-outside" tension. Because CCIs generally have foundation funding, the technical staff may work from a different perspective than do community residents. Tension can be generated between residents and nonresidents, among ethnic groups, and among people of different occupations. Specific areas of inside-outside potential conflict include

Expert skills versus local empowerment: Assigning a professional to a project may strain community building. Mechanisms to involve the community in the selection of technical experts may defuse potential friction.

Imported standards versus local goals: The desire to demonstrate success from the perspective of the funder may conflict with more personal definitions of success on the part of residents.

Representativeness versus effectiveness: Although community residents may initially slow the process as they learn to participate in governing boards, funders must seek ways to include them in formal community representation.[25]

Recognition of the need for community collaboration in national initiatives may be found in the "Model for Community Programming and Evaluation" produced by the Community National Outcomes Work Group, State Strengthening Projects, supported by CYFAR (Children, Youth, and Families at Risk).[26] The CYFAR New Communities

Project began in May 2000 and will continue and build on the work of successful participants in the State Strengthening Projects. It is an initiative that seeks to foster changes in community group processes and community structures through a framework of collaboration. This national collaborative framework characterizes the need for community building as grounded in vision to endure: "Regardless what the catalyst may be, it is critical to move from problem driven to vision driven, from muddled roles and responsibilities to defined relationships and from activity driven to outcome focused."[27]

Taken as a whole, the move to a more comprehensive approach to community building is an indicator that the next decade will find those engaged in these activities compelled to focus on holistic change rather than specific outcomes. In his analysis of systems reform in Indianapolis, Indiana, and Charlotte, North Carolina, William R. Potapchuk notes that this need to take a systems approach is affecting local governments:

> Progress on social and community development issues is no longer measured by a local government's ability to obtain federal grants and keep the peace among community groups. Whether the results of a deliberate decision to change or an accumulation of pilot programs and short-term experiments that worked, local governments today are collaborating with community organizations, nonprofits, and private industry on comprehensive approaches to all types of community issues.[28]

Public libraries are part of local government, yet their footprint on the documents, plans, and policies generated by CCIs, CDCs, Enterprise and Empowerment Zones, and State Strengthening Projects is minimal. The challenge to librarians is to become connected to these types of comprehensive community-based programs in ways that will be realized in community building assessments.

Where Do Libraries Fit?

As agencies of local governments, libraries are not generally perceived by community builders as potential participants in comprehensive community initiatives. In an overview of community building themes by the National Community Building Network, the only mention of libraries notes, "Even things you do not control (hospitals, vacant land, schools, libraries) can become your assets if you plan and partner to take advantage of them."[29]

Although this might seem discouraging, it may simply be that libraries are viewed by the broader community building movement as partners on various projects, not as integral to comprehensive community change. This supposition is supported by the paucity of reference to libraries in the literature reviewed, the foundations contacted, and the Web sites searched. Two important boundary-spanning community building organizations that do not include librarians among community building partners are the National Community Building Network and the Community Tool Box.

No library associations and no libraries are members of the National Community Building Network (NCBN), an alliance of individuals and organizations that work to reduce poverty and expand economic opportunity through comprehensive community building strategies.[30] The NCBN, founded in 1993 with support from the John D. and Catherine T. MacArthur Foundation, the Surdna Foundation, and others, is a nationwide learning community for community practitioners and researchers, in which community-based actors assist one another with problem-solving strategies. National initiatives and policy areas are monitored by the NCBN to provide influence from a community building perspective. A forum for community builders, committed to developing tools and building community capacity, the NCBN focuses on developing strong networks to connect neighborhoods with schools, businesses, faith-based organizations, civic groups, and government agencies. The theme of the 1999 NCBN annual conference was "Balancing and Using Power through Community Building."[31] Clearly, the NCBN shares many of the same goals as libraries and library associations, yet libraries are absent from the network's discussions.

The Community Tool Box is a Web site at the University of Kansas maintained by the KU Work Group on Health Promotion and Community Development, supported by the Robert Wood Johnson Foundation and the Kansas Health Foundation, that provides community building tools to connect people with the resources and information they need to make communities healthier and safer places to live. Many of the books, articles, and Web sites reviewed for this volume directed those involved in the community building movement to the Community Tool Box site as an essential resource to begin the process of comprehensive development.

The health of communities as defined by the Work Group on Health Promotion and Community Development "means children who are loved unconditionally, fed generously, and kept free from illness with immunizations and health care. It means women who do not need to fear being beaten, raped, or denied opportunities because of their gender. It means clean water and affordable housing, and peace in our neighborhoods. It means an end to racism, homophobia, and religious discrimination. It means everyone has the opportunity for decent education and jobs."[32]

Among the substantial resources available in the Community Tool Box (more than three thousand downloadable pages) only eighteen are of libraries. An analysis of the site for references about libraries produces the following number of mentions for library topics:

- Library as a place to obtain information on community demographics or history (5)
- Library as a meeting place (3)
- Library as a place to post notices or newsletters (2)
- Library as a place to obtain lists of community organizations (2)
- Library as a place to find a helpful reference librarian (2)
- Library as a place for access to a public-use computer (1)
- Library as a location for voter registration (1)
- Library as a place to obtain signatures on a petition (1)
- Library as a place to find out about grants (1)

These references to the role that libraries might play in community building (as characterized by professional community builders who develop and use this site) reflect a supportive but passive role for the library. Those who developed the Community Tool Box include professionals from public health, social services, juvenile justice, and planning agencies at all levels of government.

Yet public libraries provide service at 16,047 outlets throughout the United States, employ 117,812 staff, and spend $5.5 billion annually.[33] This public investment in the services that libraries provide demonstrates that the public is willing to pay taxes for library services and that fiscal support has grown over the years. Why do public libraries, which enjoy such broad support, fail to emerge as key participants in the literature of community building?

The answer is twofold. First, library services, no matter how energetically librarians have promoted them, are not well understood by community building organizations. Lack of understanding on the part of community builders does not mean that libraries have been overlooked. The Asset-based Community Development Institute, for example, includes libraries among community assets. Writing of the need for community change to begin from within, Institute codirectors John P. Kretzmann and John L. McKnight observe,

> Wherever there are effective community development efforts, those efforts are based upon an understanding, or map of the community's assets, capacities and abilities. . . . The key to community regeneration, then, is to locate all of the available local assets, to begin connecting them with one another in ways that multiply their power and effectiveness, and to begin harnessing those local institutions that are not yet available for local development purposes.[34]

Connecting libraries to community organizations is the way to multiply the effectiveness of libraries in building community.

Second, librarians and libraries have not been integrally involved with community visioning efforts and thus have not been identified as part of the comprehensive community building strategies being developed today. The lack of librarian participants among the rosters of community visioning projects means that the library message is not being received.

And yet, as will be seen in chapter 4, the work librarians do on a daily basis clearly fits into community building activities.

ENDNOTES

1. School library media centers and academic libraries are also central to their respective communities—elementary and secondary schools, and colleges and universities. Strategic planning in these venues is usually tied to accreditation. Regional accrediting agencies for elementary and secondary schools provide criteria that include school library media resources and personnel. For example, the standards of the North Central Association Commission on Schools identify criteria for school library media centers. Accessed November 20, 1999. Available *<http://www.nca.asu.edu/ standard/emsu/ra.html#RA_40>*. There are also regional accrediting agen-

cies for colleges and universities that include in their criteria statements about libraries and library services. See, for example, the Middle States Commission on Higher Education's "Characteristics of Excellence in Higher Education: Standards for Accreditation." Accessed November 20, 1999. Available <*http://www.msache.org/charexcl.html*>.

2. Gerald E. Frug, *City Making: Building Communities without Building Walls* (Princeton, N.J.: Princeton University Press, 1999).

3. Ibid., 219.

4. Ethel Himmel and William James Wilson with the ReVision Committee of the Public Library Association, *Planning for Results: A Public Library Transformation Process* (Chicago: American Library Association, 1998), v.

5. Ibid., 19.

6. Ibid., 20.

7. Ibid., 21.

8. World Commission on Environment and Development, *Our Common Future* (Brundtland Report) (Oxford, England; New York: Oxford University Press, 1987), 8–9.

9. President's Council on Sustainable Development, "Overview, Mission." Created in June 1993 by Executive Order 12852. Administered as a federal advisory committee under the Federal Advisory Committee Act. Accessed November 22, 1999. Available <*http://www.whitehouse.gov/PCSD/ index. html*>.

10. "From Classroom to Community and Beyond: Report of the Public Linkage, Dialogue, and Education Task Force of the President's Council on Sustainable Development." Accessed January 20, 2000. Available <*http:// www.whitehouse.gov/PCSD/Publications/TF_Reports/linkage-top.html*>.

11. President's Council on Sustainable Development, *Sustainable Communities Task Force Report* (Washington, D.C.: GPO, 1998), 7, 10.

12. President's Council on Sustainable Development, *Towards a Sustainable America: Advancing Prosperity, Opportunity, and a Healthy Environment for the 21st Century* (Washington, D.C.: GPO, 1999), 79.

13. Marie D. Hoff, "Common Themes and Replicable Strategies," in *Sustainable Community Development: Studies in Economic, Environmental, and Cultural Revitalization,* ed. Marie D. Hoff (Boca Raton, Fla.: Lewis Publishers, 1998), 230.

14. Chicago, Illinois, Empowerment Zone. Accessed November 21, 1999. Available <*http://www.ezec.gov/ezec/IL/il.html*>.

15. City of Philadelphia, Philadelphia City Planning Commission. Accessed November 21, 1999. Available <*http://www.libertynet.org/philplan/pubinfo/ overview.html*>.

16. Livable Tucson. Accessed November 21, 1999. Available <*http://www.ci. tucson.as.us/livable.html#process*>.

17. Christopher Plein, Kenneth E. Green, and David G. Williams, "Organic Planning: A New Approach to Public Participation in Local Governance," *Social Science Journal* 35, no. 4 (1998): 509–523.

18. Bryan T. Downes, "The Role of Governments in 21st Century Governance," *Social Science Journal* 35, no. 4 (1998): 589–600.

19. Aspen Institute, *Voices from the Field: Learning from the Early Work of Comprehensive Community Initiatives* (Washington, D.C.: Aspen Institute, 1997), 5.

20. Anne C. Kubisch et al., "Introduction," in *New Approaches to Evaluating Community Initiatives: Concepts, Methods, and Contexts,* ed. James P. Connell et al. (Washington, D.C.: Aspen Institute, 1995), 1–7.

21. Norman J. Glickman and Lisa J. Servon, *More Than Bricks and Sticks: What Is Community Development Capacity?* Working Paper no. 132 (New Brunswick, N.J.: Center for Urban Policy Research, Rutgers, The State University of New Jersey, 1997).

22. "Basic Facts about United Way," United Way home page. Accessed November 26, 1999. Available <*http://www.unitedway.org/bfact.htm*>.

23. United Way of America, *Achieving and Measuring Community Outcomes: Challenges, Issues, and Some Approaches* (Alexandria, Va.: United Way of America, April 1999), 2.

24. United Way of America, *Community Status Reports and Targeted Community Interventions: Drawing a Distinction: A White Paper on Change in the United Way Movement* (Alexandria, Va.: United Way of America, 1999), 4.

25. Aspen Institute, *Voices from the Field,* 21–53.

26. It is also important to be apprised of the considerable support given community building through the U.S. Department of Agriculture under the Cooperative State Research, Education and Extension Service. The State Strengthening Projects launched in 1994 under the community-based projects for Children, Youth, and Families at Risk (CYFAR) project have funded actions at 561 sites in 282 communities for 56,077 youth (ages 5–19) and 15,297 parents. These projects call for a holistic approach, viewing the individual in the context of the family and the community. Accessed November 26, 1999. Available <*http://www.reeusda.gov/new/4h/cyfar/stst/ stst2_fm.htm*>.

27. "Collaboration Framework: Addressing Community Capacity." Accessed November 26, 1999. Available <*http://www.uvm.edu/nnco/collab/frame work.html*>.

28. William R. Potapchuk, "Systems Reform in Two Cities," *National Civic Review* 87 (fall 1998): 213.

29. "Community Building Themes," National Community Building Network. Accessed November 28, 1999. Available <*http://www.ncbn.org/docs/AboutNCBN/community/index.htm*>.

30. "About the National Community Building Network." Accessed November 28, 1999. Available <*http://www.ncbn.org/docs/AboutNCBN/index.htm*>.

31. *Community Visions* 6 (spring 1999).

32. "Community Tool Box: Bringing Solutions to Light." Accessed November 23, 1999. Available <*http://www.ctb.lsi.ukans.edu/assistance/why.html*>.

33. U.S. Department of Education, *Public Libraries in the United States: FY 1996*, NCES-272, by Adrienne Chute and Elaine Kroe, National Center for Education Statistics (Washington, D.C.: USDOE, 1998).

34. John P. Kretzmann and John L. McKnight, *Building Communities from the Inside Out: A Path toward Finding and Mobilizing a Community's Assets* (Evanston, Ill.: Institute for Policy Research, 1993).

4 Factors for Successful Community Building
How the Work of Librarians Fits

Libraries and librarians build community, although this is not recognized in the broad literature of community building. The foregoing chapters have examined the dimensions of community, examined the challenges of diversity, reviewed the community visioning process, and summarized the movement toward comprehensive community building. Though libraries are seldom included in the national dialogue on community building, it is the purpose of this chapter to demonstrate that the work librarians do fits within the broad definitions as outlined in the literature. The disparity between what libraries and librarians do and how their good work is recognized needs remedy. This chapter delineates the factors that make community building work. The intention is to create common understanding by portraying the work of librarians and libraries within the context of the community building terminology.

Factors Influencing Successful Community Building

It is helpful to impose some order on the immense topic of community building to see how libraries fit. In an effort to develop a useful document for strengthening communities, Paul Mattessich and Barbara

Monsey of the Wilder Foundation reviewed 525 studies and selected 48 for analysis. These 48 were selected based on their

identification of factors that influenced the success of community building in an effort to increase community social capacity

use of empirical data demonstrating a measure of success

employment of a research methodology that demonstrated a careful case study analysis or an experimental design with control groups, statistical analysis, and reliable data collection

documentation of methodology sufficient to determine that data related to conclusions.[1]

This analysis netted twenty-eight factors that influence the success of community building.[2] These factors are discussed in this chapter. Librarians and libraries are not identified by Mattessich and Monsey as contributing to community building. There is not a single example of libraries or librarians as a resource. However, a review of these factors brings to mind a role for librarians and libraries in the context of each one. To demonstrate how naturally the work of librarians fits into community building, examples of the roles that could be played by the librarian are provided for each factor discussed. Because it is librarians who will make this happen, it is the librarian's role that is used as an example. These factors fall into three broad areas: (1) characteristics of the community, (2) characteristics of the community building process, and (3) characteristics of community building organizers.[3]

Characteristics of the Community

To build community, the community must have coherence. Successful community building initiatives will have the following factors in place:

Community Awareness of an Issue. Community building generally begins when residents recognize the need for an initiative and decide to act.

Example: Young adults of working parents have nowhere to go after school. Misdemeanor crime has increased as well as teen pregnancy.

Librarian's role: Attend community meeting, listen, and participate in offering some solutions.

Motivation from within the Community. Successful community building occurs when motivation is self-imposed rather than encouraged from outside.

Example: The county parks and recreation department decides that new lights are needed for a baseball field in a Latino community and calls a meeting to encourage community residents to have a fund-raiser.

Librarian's role: Attend community meeting. Bring information showing that the area's Latino children prefer soccer; bring specifications for soccer field.

Small Geographic Area. Successful community building occurs in coherent geographic areas where planning and implementing activities are more manageable.

Example: Broad areas without common concerns may not coalesce around an issue. A neighborhood wishing to preserve its main street appearance is unlikely to gain funding support or interest from nearby deed-restricted gated developments.

Librarian's role: Attend community meeting. Provide maps of area and local history files.

Flexibility and Adaptability. Community building efforts must be adaptable. Alternative methods must be reviewed in case one direction appears to be failing.

Example: A large regional mall is going to be built in an undeveloped area. The legal sale has been completed. Although community members meet to plan a protest, it is too late.

Librarian's role: Attend community meeting. Provide information about the new urbanist planning approach that provides an opportunity for community members to speak up about plans for new developments.

Preexisting Social Cohesion. Community building is more successful when a community spirit of problem solving exists. Community capacity can be increased more easily if these ties exist.

Example: A neighborhood has a great deal of transience because of the high number of apartment complexes. People don't show up for meetings or to rally around issues.

Librarian's role: Identify general interest programs about community issues that can be held in the library's meeting room to begin to build social cohesion among residents.

Ability to Discuss, Reach Consensus, and Cooperate. Where a spirit of cooperation already exists, there is more likely to be a basis for community problem solving.

Example: Community residents have no history of working together on common problems. When they do meet about the need for a traffic light at an increasingly busy intersection there is discussion, but no action.

Librarian's role: Attend community meeting. Provide information from traffic analysis studies and review transportation department actions and procedures, perhaps including an example of a success elsewhere under the same governance structure.

Existing Identifiable Leadership. Often the catalyst for community problem solving is someone in a position of leadership—scouting, faith-based, sports—who can generate support.

Example: A countywide opportunity for a beautification grant was missed by a low-income community because there was no one to step forward and develop an application.

Librarian's role: On hearing a library user express disappointment about this missed opportunity, the librarian invited several officers of community clubs to stop by the library for coffee and to talk together about the issue and offered the use of the library's meeting room.

Prior Success with Community Building. The obvious is true—experience counts. Yet what if the community has never initiated an effort to solve its problems?

Example: A rural community is losing its downtown stores to a Wal-Mart. Residents want to keep the old downtown, but prices are so much lower at the new chain store. No one knows where to begin.

Librarian's role: The librarian sets up a display in the library of main streets that coexist with big box stores and provides books about the process. She contacts the county extension agent to provide a program.

Characteristics of the Community Building Process

The more of the following characteristics that are present in the process of community building, the more likely the process will be successful.

> *Widespread Participation.* Participants should represent all or most segments of the community and must be recruited continuously. This will bring in the talents and resources of a wider, more diverse group, increase the likelihood of political acceptability, and help create ties to outsiders who may contribute resources or control the environment that can affect the success of the effort.
>
> *Example:* The civic association attracts longtime neighborhood residents, but no young families attend.
>
> *Librarian's role:* Attend county meeting. Provide a storytime (even off-site if the meeting is held elsewhere than the library) so that parents of young children can attend.
>
> *Good System of Communication.* Communication ensures that all residents of a community remain aware and motivated, serving to maintain widespread participation.
>
> *Example:* An urban neighborhood with many challenges, such as a crumbling infrastructure, high unemployment, and no after-school programs for children, is seldom covered in the city newspaper and has no local newspaper.
>
> *Librarian's role:* The library maintains a Web page of community events that can be printed off as a flyer and distributed to laundromats, health clinics, and churches.
>
> *Minimal Competition in Pursuit of Goals.* Sometimes there are several community groups with similar activities. A collaboration should be developed to build on each other's strengths rather than compete for limited resources.
>
> *Example:* The YMCA and Big Brothers and Big Sisters decide to provide homework help programs.
>
> *Librarian's role:* Provide a quiet area for after-school tutoring without differentiating between the organizations and have staff "on-call" for assistance as needed.

Develop Self-Understanding. Development of a group identity helps clarify priorities and achieve goals.

Example: Many frail elderly living alone feel isolated and unconnected. The various elder care organizations unite to serve them systematically.

Librarian's role: Attend the elder care meeting and provide a list of community resources, including books-by-mail, to demonstrate that access is available.

Benefits to Many Residents. The most successful community building reaches out to the most residents.

Example: Community cleanup pulls together middle school and high school students, service organizations, environmental groups, and civic associations.

Librarian's role: Staff the sign-in booth for the community cleanup and provide information on safety while cleaning the roadsides, brochures on plants, and recycling information.

Focus on Product and Process Concurrently. Successful community building focuses on tasks but also pays attention to organizing and bringing new residents into the process.

Example: The community has come together to have the city install streetlights. A committee has been assigned to work with the city. Those not on the committee begin to lose interest.

Librarian's role: Provide a map in the library showing successful project locations and provide information that a planning committee might review next.

Linkage to Organizations Outside the Community. Ties to organizations outside the community can help in identifying financial support, political support, sources of knowledge, and technical support.

Example: Community residents, noting that other communities in the region have new recreation centers, are unsure how to initiate their own efforts to build such a facility.

Librarian's role: Of all the factors yet discussed, this one is the most natural for a librarian—especially sources of knowledge.

The librarian can seek out information that helps reduce community isolation and provide it for community meetings.

Progression from Simple to Complex Activities

Example: A community organizes holiday decorations and a tree lighting. Based on cooperation skills developed through this process, the group decides to work for community improvement.

Librarian's role: Obtain community association bylaws and newsletters from other groups in the area as examples.

Systematic Gathering of Information and Analysis of Community Issues. Gathering information about problems helps successful community building occur.

Example: Grants have been made available to develop a better health care infrastructure for communities in need. Although residents perceive that health care is a problem for their community, they have no reliable data.

Librarian's role: Use census data on income to help assemble a background report.

Training to Gain Community Building Skills. Successful community building efforts are more likely to occur when the participants have some training or background in developing and maintaining an organization.

Example: A new civic association is having difficulty attracting and keeping members.

Librarian's role: Identify sources of support from such organizations as the Civic Practices Network—either printed material or possible trainer volunteers.

Early Involvement and Support from Existing, Indigenous Organizations. New community building efforts can be sustained if established contacts, leaders of extant organizations, and existing resources contribute to the new effort.

Example: A teen-pregnancy prevention program seems important to the parents of young adults. To begin this program, they call on faith-based organization leaders, the PTA, and the scouting volunteers.

Librarian's role: Provide a list of additional community organizations that might be allied with the initiative.

Use of Technical Assistance. Technical assistance can be helpful for specific problems (zoning regulations) or for general community building (leadership development).

Example: A large old house that residents wish to turn into a community center is for sale. Residents need information about zoning and licensing.

Librarian's role: Provide a list of governmental entities that oversee zoning and licensing. Again, the search for technical assistance could very well be done by a librarian, but suggestions for seeking this help do not mention the library as a source.

Continual Emergence of Leaders As Needed. Community building efforts that encourage different participants to take leadership roles are stronger than those with one charismatic leader.

Example: An organization formed to stop the destruction of a small river because of fertilizer runoff was bolstered by a strong environmentalist who later moved from the area. Although other environmental issues needed addressing, no one came to the plate to continue these efforts.

Librarian's role: Provide ongoing displays and programs in the library on environmental issues to keep up interest and perhaps draw a new leader.

Community Control over Decision Making. When residents have control over decisions and funds, success is more likely.

Example: The local civic association received a small grant from the county to develop a community newsletter, but purchase order and reporting requirements took so much time away from the actual project that the community gave it up.

Librarian's role: Provide information about becoming an independent organization through state and federal guidelines.

The Right Mix of Resources. Too many resources as well as not enough resources can make community building difficult.

Example: As community building begins, small amounts of funds can make it possible to plan and execute small projects. Additional resources are better used as there is sufficient experience to use them well.

Librarian's role: Identify grant-funding opportunities with evaluation of suitability for the community.

Characteristics of Community Building Organizers

Community building organizers—those who lead community building efforts—will understand their community, be sincere, build trust, have organizing experience, and be flexible and adaptable. The librarian thus can be defined as a true community builder.

UNDERSTANDING THE COMMUNITY

Community building is best done when organizers understand the community's culture (belief patterns, social norms, significant traditions), social structure (existing social networks), demographics (age groups, ethnicity, housing patterns), political structures (formal and informal power), and major issues of concern to the community. The librarian can demonstrate community understanding through developing the collection and programs for different segments of the community.

SINCERITY OF COMMITMENT

To be successful, community builders must be interested in the community's long-term well-being, must have a sustained commitment to community members, must be honest, and must be committed to the community rather than to an external group. The librarian, whether hired by the community, or assigned to work in a given community, can attend vital community meetings, provide information, and work for the needs of the geographic area by joining community associations and assisting them with their work.

A RELATIONSHIP OF TRUST

There are many elements to building a trusting relationship. These include commitment to a common mission, impartial treatment of all community members, and following through on promises. As a community builder, the librarian will assume tasks that can be completed, provide information equally for all sides of issues, and try to understand community goals.

ORGANIZING EXPERIENCE

Successful community builders need experience. Librarians who understand how communities work, who view their work in the community as part of the infrastructure of the neighborhood, and who recognize when they can make a useful contribution to civic improvement will be more successful than the librarian who sees library work as interchangeable regardless of location.

FLEXIBILITY AND ADAPTABILITY

Flexibility and adaptability are essential in community building. The ability to adapt to the needs of the community in which the librarian works is central to success.

Librarians Building Community

The factors discussed in this chapter are required to build community. They will help develop and sustain strong relationships. They will increase problem-solving and decision-making skills. They will improve the ability to collaborate effectively to identify goals and get work done.[4]

Most librarians work to build community. They may not characterize their daily work in these terms but the result of their work is fundamental to the development of strong community capacity. To identify examples of librarians working to build community, I contacted staff at national, state, and local organizations that focus their energies on community building. Many had not thought of libraries and librarians as central to the community building effort, and the literature reviewed bears this out. However, messages to community building electronic discussion groups and calls to organizations did result in the identification of librarians whose contributions were known to community building workers. Clearly many librarians work within the community building model, but there is no recognition within the network of community builders that librarians can be central to these efforts. The five stories of librarians who build community presented in the next chapter represent us all.

ENDNOTES

1. Paul Mattessich and Barbara Monsey, *Community Building: What Makes It Work* (St. Paul, Minn.: Amherst H. Wilder Foundation, 1997), 65–70.
2. The selection of the Mattessich and Monsey matrix is based upon a comprehensive review of the broad community building literature and the suitability of this matrix for librarians who want to build community.
3. Mattessich and Monsey, 19–49.
4. Ibid., 3.

5

Librarians Who
Build Community
Voices from the Front Lines

How do librarians build community? Taking into consideration the various factors discussed in the previous chapters and moving to identify community building characteristics that fit these factors, five librarians and their staffs were selected as case studies of community builders. They were selected because their work was recommended by external community building professionals or organizers of community building projects, such as the CYFAR initiative (Children, Youth, and Families at Risk), the Civic League, Community Development Corporations, the Rural Social Services Partnership, and the National Endowment for the Humanities. A profile of the community and responses by library staff to community building questions is presented for each library. Certainly, no brief overview can do justice to the complete scope of the work done by these librarians, but their responses to challenges in the context of an active community building worldview helps to demonstrate the focus of this book.

All the librarians, of course, felt they were doing what they should be doing—that the work they were doing was not different from the work that all librarians do. Of course, this is, to some degree, true. Aspects of community building are inherent in the work of all public librarians. However, the fact that the work of these librarians was viewed by external community builders as exemplary was cause for inclusion. An aim of this volume is that the work librarians do be seen as integral to their communities by all members of community building initiatives. By reviewing the work of these librarians and their responses to community building issues, the library profession can derive a broader understanding of what it means to build community.

Each librarian was asked the following questions:

1. What are examples of community activities in which you are involved outside the library?
2. How does your community involvement affect the services delivered at your library?
3. Based on our discussion of community building, what makes you a community builder?
4. If you are not the chief administrator of your library, how does your library's administration support community building?

E. ANNETTE CHOSZCZYK
Glendale Public Library
(Glendale, Colorado <http://www.glendale.co.us/library/>)

Glendale, Colorado, is an island completely surrounded by Denver. This home-rule city has a daytime population of 35,000, but only 4,200 full-time residents. The Glendale Public Library is a full-service branch of the Arapahoe Regional Library District.

In 1988, the Glendale Library had one staff member and was housed in a temporary classroom with limited hours. At that time, changes in immigration and refugee rules brought many Russian-speaking refugee families into the neighborhood around the library, including a library manager from the former Soviet Union who volunteered to help the Glendale Library serve these new arrivals. An LSCA grant allowed development of a popular Russian-language collection and the addition of English as a second language and vocational collections. English classes began to meet around the library's only table, and the library desperately needed room for expansion. A collaborative effort with the City of Glendale allowed the library to relocate to the fourth floor of the Glendale Community Center in 1990, and an additional LSCA grant made possible the purchase of more materials and the addition of the Russian-speaking volunteer as a paid staff member. By 1999, the Denver-area population of Russian-speaking immigrants was more than 30,000, and the library and staff and hours expanded to meet their needs.

Currently the Glendale Public Library is a full-service bilingual branch library with Russian-speaking staff available to assist patrons during all open hours. More than 60 percent of library use is by Russian-speaking patrons. The following services and programs are offered:

English as a Second Language (ESL) classes in partnership with the Spring Institute of International Studies and the Office of Refugee Resettlement, Colorado Department of Education, the City of Glendale, and private donations. Most students (85–90 percent) are Russian-speaking.

English conversation groups. Volunteers hold classes for those wishing to practice English skills.

Citizenship tutoring. Russian-language collections, including books for all ages, magazines, newspapers, cassettes, and videos.

ESL and vocational materials collections on careers, business, educational opportunities, and job search strategies.

Translated programs on topics of interest, such as income tax preparation, insurance, social security, Medicaid, credit and mortgages, buying a car.

Referral information.

Programming that bridges cultural and language gaps for children and adults.

The library's services and circulation have escalated over the past few years. In 1994, circulation totaled 5,628; in 1995, after the move to the new facility, it was 55,648, growing 25–32 percent each year. Growth of this magnitude and the ability to respond to the needs of a diverse community require careful attention to community building on the part of staff. Librarian E. Annette Choszczyk responded to the community building questions:

1. Community activities include the following:

Glendale Family Center: I have been on the planning committee for the Family Center Initiative and its governing board since it was funded. The Family Center serves low-income individuals and families with emergency food, referrals to other social services, weekly and monthly food banks, and advocacy for Spanish speakers. To some extent, family centers—located throughout

Colorado—play the same role the library should play. I attended the State-Wide Family Center meeting and the Glendale Library was featured in an article about Family Center/Library Collaboration by the National Family Center Initiative.[1]

Glendale 2000 Planning Process.

Glendale Area Service Providers: Monthly meeting of school district, Family Center, police, fire, and library staff.

Science, Arts, and Sports Center for Children: Worked on initial grant-writing for funding; library provides space for programming on enrichment classes for Russian immigrant children.

Glendale Master Plan: The city's planning and space use project.

Glendale Charter School Planning Process: Planning committee to consider a charter school.

New school and recreation center planning process.

Tutoring program: Helped seek funding for after-school and homework support for community children.

Glendale Business Association.

Four Mile Historic Park.

Refugee Provider Service Meetings.

New Community Music School.

2. Community involvement greatly affects the way my library serves our community. Keeping in close contact with the trends and needs in the community, networking with major players, and finding out about the needs of our population are critical. Much credit goes to the assistant librarian, Diana Dvorkina, the Russian-speaking librarian who was a library manager in the former Soviet Union and who came to the area as a refugee. She is part of the culture we serve and has helped me build a truly bilingual facility. She has contacts from Glendale to Washington and will not stop until she has the answer to a question as she has helped to build a referral bank for those new to the country. Together we have built these services from scratch—a true collaboration and labor of love.

3. Libraries are community centers and I believe librarians can be vital to our communities. I feel driven to provide our patrons that which is real and important to them. Libraries embody some of the finest aspects of the United States—free access to information; free use

of equipment; free help of people trained to answer questions. Libraries really do provide service and information to all who enter, and that makes all the difference.

When coming to our English classes helps to give meaning to the life of a suicidal elderly woman; when Diana's intervention helps obtain life-saving health care for a very sick child; when five hundred elderly Russian-speaking patrons get help with state tax refunds; when people trust us to help them with the hardest problems of their lives—we are making a difference. Yes, we do the usual things a library does, but we get to do so much more, which enriches our lives, and our use just keeps growing.

I love to develop things and try out new ideas and am always looking for new ways to be involved in the community and new collaborations to make. Everything around me in my community is part of my work. I love being involved in cross-cultural exchanges.

My warning is that a library that reaches out to the needs of the community will be used—and more than you can guess! If it is an immigrant community and you can serve patrons in their own languages and with culturally appropriate materials, programs, and services, you will be amazed at the response.

As library work goes, this is the best for me. I love the ability of a smaller-sized library to make a real impact on a neighborhood. Even though our circulation has grown 1,500 percent, we are still not too big and my staff really know our patrons and they know us. We have become the beloved deli in a city full of big supermarkets. I love being the deli . . . we can experiment more, we can innovate more, and we can really respond to our patrons.

MARGARET STEINFURTH and RODRIGO DIAZ
Ruskin Branch Library
(Ruskin, Florida <http://scfn.thpl.lib.fl.us/thpl/libraries/
  branch/rus/rus.htm>)

Ruskin, Florida, is an unincorporated area in south Hillsborough County. Although the county includes the city of Tampa, the southern portion of the county is rural with primary industries of tomato and citrus growing and packing. These activities attract a large population of seasonal farmworkers, mostly from Mexico. Although it is difficult to ascertain an exact number, the county estimates that there are 26,000 seasonal farmworkers in the Ruskin area. A large retirement community of affluent elderly, Sun City Center, is also nearby.

Margaret Steinfurth, principal librarian, and Rodrigo Diaz, librarian, are the only two full-time librarians at the Ruskin Branch of the Tampa–Hillsborough County Public Library System. They work collaboratively on community building.

1. *Margaret Steinfurth:* I regularly attend meetings of the Ruskin Civic Association, the Ruskin Chamber of Commerce, the Ruskin Community Development Foundation, the South County President's Roundtable (although the library is in Ruskin, our service area is all of "south" county and the President's Roundtable is a coalition of civic and community associations from the entire area), and town meetings sponsored by the county's Office of Neighborhood Relations.

Ruskin serves an area that is primarily agricultural, and the widespread development that has taken place in other parts of the county nearer to Tampa has not yet begun in force here. The library is located on an inlet that flows into Tampa Bay, and I have worked with an environmental group, "The Pepper Patrol" (named after the nonnative invasive Brazilian Pepper Plant that has spread throughout the area's wetlands) to eradicate nonnative plants and to plant native vegetation. The plants have signage and the area around the library provides an experience of the original Florida habitat. Egrets, fish, and manatees may be seen near the library.

I patronize local stores—Ruskin still has some mom-and-pop businesses—and provide a library presence at events like the Ruskin Tomato Festival and the Ruskin Sea Food Festival.

Rodrigo Diaz: My outreach activities lead me to contacts and opportunities for programming and penetration into the community. Organizations with which I have worked include those focusing on migrant workers and their families—as a Spanish speaker I have cultural skills to work effectively with these patrons (Bethune Park Recreation Center, Iglesia de Dios Success Center, Ruskin Migrant Infant Center, Ruskin Migrant Head Start, Estancia Migrant Head Start, San Jose Mission, Beth-El Farm Worker Mission). Other community groups include Adult Day Care Center; Ruskin Health Center; elementary, middle, and secondary schools; and the Probation and Parole Board.

2. *Margaret Steinfurth:* Frequent contact with community groups helps the library respond to current needs. Our support of community

development through distribution of literature has been highlighted in local newspapers and has enhanced the community's view of the library as an information center.

Rodrigo Diaz: My contacts with local social service and education providers have given me an understanding of the needs of the migrant population and youth at risk. I have involved the after-school and Head Start programs in library card sign-ups and conducted "back-to-school" programs where I provided information for adults about library services. I have made presentations about library services at community fairs.

3. *Margaret Steinfurth:* My entire family was devoted to social service as teachers, librarians, ministers. I worked thirteen years as a county social service worker before becoming a librarian. I consciously chose a profession that would have a community service component.

Rodrigo Diaz: I was born and raised in Tampa, Florida, where my grandparents had come from Cuba to work in the city's cigar industry. While they rolled cigars they listened to the lector, who read great works by Emile Zola, Victor Hugo, Cervantes. They contributed twenty-five cents a week to have the lector read to them, as did all the cigar rollers.[2] Thus, in my family, the love of reading was a value we cherished.

In college, I majored in philosophy and was greatly influenced by the writing of John Rawls, especially *A Theory of Justice.*[3] I joined the Peace Corps and served in the Dominican Republic. There I saw the desire of people to read and learn. When I returned to Tampa and enrolled at the University of South Florida School of Library and Information Science to be a librarian, I studied the needs of farmworkers and realized that a librarian with Spanish-language skills would serve this community well. Upon graduation I was employed by the Tampa–Hillsborough County Public Library System and was assigned to work in Ruskin, a community with great need for outreach in Spanish.

My family's commitment to learning and my personal commitment to helping others to read and benefit from knowledge have combined to encourage me to reach out where the library is needed.

4. *Joe Stines,* Library Director: Tampa–Hillsborough is a geographically large library system with twenty-two branches, three regional libraries, and a large central library. It includes urban Tampa, suburban areas, and agricultural areas. Communities in the Tampa–Hillsborough Library System service area are experiencing change and growth. In

some areas, growth threatens the small-town feeling and the concept of home rule. Librarians who participate in neighborhood civic associations, resident councils, and leadership groups, such as the South County President's Roundtable, are in a position to be part of the change process.

The library is often a facility that provides stability to a community; it is one of the service centers that citizens can call their own. With an atmosphere of accessibility, proximity, and security, the library is meaningful for the community as a whole.

In the area of our county served by the Ruskin Public Library, librarians partner with the community in more ways than just working with organizations. Librarians analyze the community to gain knowledge of the language barriers, economic barriers, and educational barriers that make it difficult for new residents to participate in community life.

The knowledge librarians gain through community involvement combined with proactive roles in outreach can make community building a success.

JEAN HATFIELD
Antioch Branch of the Johnson County Library
(Merriam, Kansas <http://www.jcl.lib.ks.us/otherlib/antioch.stm>)

Johnson County, Kansas, has a population of 307,000. The Johnson County Library service area is contiguous with the metropolitan Kansas City area and has reciprocal borrowing privileges with the libraries of Johnson County Community College; Kansas City, Kansas; Olathe, Kansas; and Kansas City, Missouri. The library was ranked as the strongest library serving a population between 250,000 and 400,000 by the Hennen American Public Library Ratings Index.[4]

The Antioch Branch is one of twelve branches and houses classrooms for Project Finish, a cooperative program with the Johnson County Community College that provides Adult Basic Education/GED classes and ESL classes.

1. I have served on the board of the Child Care Association of Johnson County, the resource and referral agency for child care providers funded through its role as the administrator for the federal funds that subsidize lunches for children in child care.

I also serve as board chair of the Economic Opportunity Corporation (EOC) of St. Joseph, Missouri, which serves a four-county area and is the parent agency for Head Start as well as providing job training, resources and referral for low-income families, and intervention for families in danger of losing their children. The EOC is also starting to get involved in providing housing for low-income families and training for people interested in starting their own small businesses. The goal of this community action agency is to help families become self-sufficient and to break the cycle of poverty.

2. My experience with the child care board and the Economic Opportunity Corporation have provided me with insight into social problems and possible solutions that may impact library services. Our outreach program was strengthened because of my experience gained in meeting early-childhood specialists and day care providers. Work with the Economic Opportunity Corporation helped me to develop expertise in recognizing the problems of families at risk, which led me to apply for national funding.

The funding the Antioch Branch received to participate in the *National Connections* project has some grounding in your community involvement. Can you describe this program?

National Connections is an adult reading and discussion program funded by the National Endowment for the Humanities and administered by the Vermont Humanities Council in collaboration with the American Library Association.[5] The program requires collaboration among librarians, adult education program staff, a scholar, and the humanities council. The collaboration among these agencies to enhance the skills of adult new readers builds community through provider networking in order to help new readers develop conceptual reading skills through the discussion of humanities themes.

3. I am simply a librarian who feels strongly that the library should be a place in which everyone in the community should feel comfortable. I feel that the best way to make connections in the community is to become involved in whatever way I can. The more a librarian knows about the community, the better the public can be served.

4. The county librarian, Mona Carmack, has encouraged my participation in community building. She has been supportive of any staff member who wishes to serve on a nonprofit board or to be actively involved in community and civic organizations. She has supported my active involvement in the formation of the Heartland Chapter of REFORMA and encourages staff to be active in professional organizations. Ms. Carmack feels that as stewards of public funds, we have an

obligation to make the best use of those funds to serve the largest number of patrons efficiently and that the more we know about our community and our profession, the better we will be able to serve our patrons.

MARY ROMEO
DeKalb Branch (Bushwick Avenue at DeKalb Avenue)
   of the Brooklyn Public Library
(Brooklyn, New York <http://www.brooklynpubliclibrary.
   org/branches/dekalb.htm>)

Brooklyn Public Library serves nearly two million Brooklyn residents at its central and business libraries and fifty-eight branches. The DeKalb Branch serves a population of more than 70,000 in the Bushwick neighborhood. Bushwick has been the focus of community development initiatives. The Bushwick Local Development Corporation has focused on community stabilization, especially in West Bushwick. The Bushwick Renaissance Mixed Use Initiative is a comprehensive strategy to link housing with job creation and economic development. Bushwick residents are among the poorest in the city, with 40.5 percent below the poverty line. The population is 81.1 percent Hispanic, 10.5 percent black non-Hispanic, and 4.7 percent white non-Hispanic.[6]

1. I am involved in many community activities, including block association parties, community agency open houses, merchant association street fairs, senior center health fairs and regional meetings, Community School Board #32 meetings, school career days, community board monthly meetings, Lawton Street Community Advisory Board meetings, and Bushwick Resource Coalition meetings.

These connections provide linkages to the community. Sometimes my involvement will provide opportunity for grant applications. Sometimes my involvement provides me with the knowledge to refer library patrons to community services or to provide literature about community services. One example is the Togetherness with Love Community Program. At our library we also do special programs for community groups, such as the Bushwick Childcare Network. By attending community events, we have become involved in the Bushwick Resource Coalition. Constant involvement in the community provides networking opportunities to serve our patrons.

2. We expect our staff to be competent in their knowledge of the neighborhood and its customers. After the last census report we real-

ized that there were huge pockets of residents that we never saw. The decision was made to make the effort to go out into the neighborhood to those areas where we felt we could make contact with these groups.

This is not an affluent neighborhood. Many grandparents provide child care while their adult children work. Thus, involvement with the senior centers provides access to families.

At senior center meetings we also realized that there were topics for possible programming that the library could provide, and we decided we could facilitate programs needed. Based on these discussions we have held programs on hair care, child care and birth control, home buying, basic computer information, Internet use for families, and fire safety.

When residents request the use of our auditorium, we use the opportunity to do book displays and encourage library card registration. Recent examples are the Magnific Sports Association, Positive Health, Togetherness with Love, Community Board #4, the Bushwick Resource Coalition, and the Bushwick Neighborhood Advisory Council.

Participating in and maintaining and improving interaction with civic and ethnic groups in the community gives us a chance to meet our patrons' needs and to learn about the community. This has had a significant impact on staff training and programming. We have been able to develop a knowledge base to deliver more customized services to our users. We have been able to demonstrate that we provide services to organizations as well as to individuals. When our patrons use the words "DeKalb library," they can easily remember or identify the person they met at a community event. This ends up being very important when we have to go to the board during the budgeting process. This becomes our forum to establish the DeKalb library as the center of neighborhood knowledge. We are able to network so that whenever groups need to connect to the community at large, they think first of making contact at the library so that we can disseminate their literature or refer them to the "right people."

3. Each community in Brooklyn is different. In some communities outreach is not as important because the culture or affluence of the community has created a captive audience. Bushwick is not such a community. Here outreach is important. In this community staff members have the opportunity to be more than just competent in this area of their skill development. Since I consider myself a formidable trainer, every opportunity is given for staff members to reach out to schools and community organizations for programming.

I understand the importance of having patrons and the community groups be able to put a face to the word *library,* so whenever an organization requests that someone from the library attend an activity, we try to accede to the request. This is vital to the economic viability of the library system during the city's budgeting process and whenever the branch needs support and help for a problem. This approach might seem opportunistic, but I think it shows political savvy. As a creative manager of limited resources, I believe it is an opportunity for us to have other groups and organizations come in and do programming for us for free!

4. Our director, Martín Goméz, is committed to the library being a "vital knowledge center for all." With this vision and a mission of providing the people of Brooklyn with twenty-four-hour access to society's knowledge, history, and culture, it was mandatory for each branch to find ways of encouraging increased usage. We have focused our outreach efforts as one way of achieving this mission and vision.

BARBARA HEIDERSCHEIDT
Avon Grove Free Library
(West Grove, Pennsylvania <http://www.ccls.org/
  otherlibs/avon.htm>)

Avon Grove Free Library is part of the Chester County Library System located in southeastern Pennsylvania. It is a federated system composed of a District Center in Exton and sixteen member libraries and a bookmobile. Avon Grove Free Library is a small-town library and serves a sixty-five-square-mile area with a population of 20,000.

The library was identified as an exemplary community partner by staff members of the U.S. Department of Agriculture's Children, Youth, and Families at Risk (CYFAR) program.[7]

1. I am involved in the following community activities: the Avon Grove Youth Serving Coalition, a community board of directors for drug and alcohol education for youth in local schools; Music Boosters at Avon Grove Public High School; the PTA at a local Catholic elementary school; and the Catholic church teen youth group.

2. The youth groups in which I participate keep me in touch with many young adults and their parents. When I hear of projects that can benefit from exposure to the library, I work hard to make this happen.

Examples include use of the Internet, use of the library as a meeting place, and the CYFAR project.

The CYFAR project targets children, youth, and families at risk and is coordinated by Penn State University Cooperative Extension. It includes a computer donated to the library and development of a program of community volunteers. I participate as a volunteer in addition to my regular library work.

Volunteers provide a series of instructions to young people and their families to help them with basic computer skills and to help them use computers to obtain information on health, budgeting, child care, homemaking, and human growth and development. This includes collaboration with the 4-H program.

Through 4-H the library has offered well-attended programs on science, crafts, and life skills. I was a lead teacher for these classes and secured additional instructors. Involvement with CYFAR and the 4-H programs has enabled me to provide more library programming.

CYFAR planning has also brought me to work in the Migrant Education Program at the local middle school to create a more personal one- or two-on-one teaching program for English as a second language. This lets me show that the library staff makes these young people welcome in our community and encourages them to use the library after school with their families.

Involvement with this program has helped me create an informal alliance with the migrants' teachers and we have worked together to offer a bilingual storytime that attracts preschool children and their mothers.

By making presentations to community groups about the library, I am able to make many connections that lead to new library service. After a presentation to the West Grove Mothers Club, I met the teacher of a class of children with disabilities and was able to participate in the service project the club was doing for these children. I was able to provide an outreach storytime and craft experience for these children. Using my network at the church, I was able to recruit teen volunteers to help.

My work with the Avon Grove Youth Serving Coalition involves training and recruiting mentors for young people. My involvement in youth church activities gives me access to potential volunteers.

3. I personally believe that a strong community makes a good place to live and raise children. I like to put people in touch with others who can benefit from more knowledge or current, innovative technology. I like

to learn new things and create coalitions of local folks who can help young people because young people are the future of our world. I have a hopeful view of the human race. I think we can work together to make our local space and our large earth a friendly place to live and to create.

Values of Librarians Who Build Community

By examining the preceding five case studies of librarians who are community builders in different settings, it is possible to identify values that contribute to the library's becoming a full partner in comprehensive initiatives.

The following shared values characterize the respondents' perceptions of library service:

Community Involvement   The more involved the librarian, the stronger the commitment to community building. Most respondents not only attend community meetings but take active roles as citizens—serving on committees and boards, assisting with grant development, providing personal skills and resources.

Awareness of Community Issues   Respondents are able to identify and articulate issues of concern to the communities in which they work. Their knowledge of these issues is at both the micro and macro levels.

Connection as a Responsibility   Librarians see their community involvement as generating new opportunities for service in direct relation to needs they are able to identify and discuss through their interaction with community members at civic, social service, and educational meetings.

Integration of Service   Librarians involved in community organizations are able to identify service integration as a key issue. They are able to understand and conceptualize the model of service from a systemic point of view rather than from a library-centric point of view. Information and referral are identified as services best activated through basic understanding of the community's structure.

Community Building as a Value   These librarians are articulate about community building and the importance of community.

They express the philosophy that a strong community is a good place to live, where concern for all people, especially youth and the elderly, is important. Libraries are seen as contributing to a better quality of life.

The Library Can Make a Difference All librarians are firm in their assessment of the role of the library in the community. By putting a face to the library at community meetings and events, these librarians feel they can connect to residents in ways that are meaningful for them. These librarians express optimism in the library as a place open to all and as a public service that can be innovative in response to people's real needs.

These values transcend the everyday approach to work. They are values that demonstrate a commitment to the kinds of concerns described in this book's opening chapters. They indicate an incorporation of the ideals of mutual responsibility for civic involvement called for in *The New Progressive Declaration: A Political Philosophy for the Information Age.*[8] The *Declaration* redefines the relationship between citizens and government, requiring that citizens be active participants in producing public goods, such as safe streets and a clean environment. This new relationship defines *public* as the domain of citizens, not just government, and it puts trust in the broad common judgments of citizens rather than the narrow expertise of technocratic elites. This approach calls for less large centralized government and more responsibility on the part of local governments, individual citizens, and community institutions for tackling public problems.

As these ideas gain strength, the need for librarians to be involved as citizens in their communities is of growing importance. Although the daily work life of many librarians, and many library vision statements, contain aspects of these values, they are by no means generally incorporated across the board. By next discussing key areas of community building in light of library service, it will be clearer how these might link together.

ENDNOTES

1. The Colorado initiative in which Ms. Choszczyk participates is a project of the Family Resource Coalition of America. Accessed January 1, 2000. Available *<http://www.frca.org>*.

2. For more information on the lector, see Ferdie Pacheco, *Art of Ybor City* (Gainesville: University of Florida, 1997), 6–11.

3. John Rawls, *A Theory of Justice* (Cambridge, Mass.: Belknap Press of Harvard University Press, 1971).

4. Thomas J. Hennen, Jr., "Great American Public Libraries," *American Libraries* 30 (September 1998): 66.

5. The *National Connections* project is described on the home page of the Vermont Humanities Council at *http://www.vermonthumanities.org/* (accessed January 1, 2000), and on the home page for public programs at the American Library Association at *http://www.ala.org/publicprograms/national/general.html* (accessed January 1, 2000).

6. Bushwick Local Development Corp., "The Bushwick Renaissance Mixed Use Initiative," sponsored by the Ridgewood Bushwick Senior Citizens Council and the Bushwick Local Development Corp. Accessed January 21, 2000. Available *<http://www.bushwickldc.org>*.

7. U.S. Department of Agriculture, Children, Youth, and Families at Risk, "Strong States and Networks for Children, Youth, and Families," home page. Accessed January 2, 2000. Available *<http://www.reeusda.gov/new/4h/cyfar/cyfar.htm>*.

8. Will Marshall et al., *The New Progressive Declaration: A Political Philosophy for the Information Age* (Washington, D.C.: Progressive Policy Institute, 1996).

6

Cybercommunity Building and Librarians

Before discussing how to connect librarians to the national movement to build community, it is important to address the role of cybercommunities and the public library. The Internet, electronic resources, the World Wide Web, and e-mail viewed as a system have generated a large body of writing and research bundled under the rubrics *cybercommunity* or *virtual community*. Many librarians, already familiar with e-mail through BITNET and with wide-scale networking through experience with online databases and OCLC, were early adapters in their own work life of the components that make up cybercommunity and have also played a strong advocacy role in ensuring Internet access to users.

First Phases
TIIAP, Community Networking, and OITP

Libraries were well represented among early rounds of grantees from the Telecommunications and Information Infrastructure Assistance Program (TIIAP) administered by the National Telecommunications and Information Administration (NTIA), which provided funds for innovative services. These libraries included San Francisco Public Library, the Southeast Florida Library Information Network (SEFLIN),

SOLINET, Bowling Green Public Library, Newark Public Library, the Public Library of Charlotte and Mecklenburg County, Danbury Public Library, Denver Public Library, Salem (Oregon) Public Library, New York Public Library, and Queens Public Library.[1]

These projects all demonstrated a keen librarian responsiveness to community needs. At Newark Public Library, funds were used to support the Newark Electronic Information Infrastructure Demonstration Project as a component of the Empowerment Zone plan (1994–1996). New York Public Library, working with the Literacy Assistance Center (LAC) of New York City, tested networked information resources at thirty neighborhood branches, encouraging people with limited literacy skills to use computer resources (1996–1999). Danbury Public Library developed a model community Freenet planning process for the state of Connecticut (1994–1995). Three counties in southeast Florida (Broward, Dade, and Palm Beach) developed a Free-Net training infrastructure coordinated by SEFLIN (1995–1996). The Salem (Oregon) Public Library developed OPEN (Oregon Public Electronic Network) to enhance the exchange of information between government and citizens and to provide the infrastructure for regional businesses and organizations to market their products and services through the World Wide Web (1995–1997).

In *The Community Networking Handbook,* Stephen T. Bajjaly has identified the library as the natural leader of the community networking effort; provided examples of successful library-initiated networks, such as the Three Rivers Free-Net; and outlined steps to plan, develop, manage, and fund networks.[2] He makes a strong case for the participation of libraries in community networking initiatives and sees that one of the profession's most important responsibilities is helping communities deal effectively with the information age.[3]

The American Library Association established the Office for Information Technology Policy (OITP) in 1995 to promote the development and utilization of electronic access to information as a means to ensure the public's right to a free and open information society.[4] The OITP staff works to secure information technology policies favorable to library services and full intellectual participation to the public. This included work to implement the Universal Service Program that was established as part of the Telecommunications Act of 1996 to provide affordable access to telecommunications services for libraries, particularly those in rural and inner-city areas.[5]

Advocacy and Access

Advocacy must be grounded in baseline information, and the National Commission on Libraries and Information Science in collaboration with the ALA OITP has sponsored data-gathering research on public libraries and the Internet. *Moving toward More Effective Public Internet Access: The 1998 National Survey of Public Library Outlet Internet Connectivity* reported that 83.6 percent of public libraries had Internet access to the public with rural libraries lagging behind those in metropolitan areas.[6] However, many of these workstations did not provide graphical access, and bandwidth was often less than 56 kbps.

The Library Services and Technology Act (LSTA) of 1996 (P.L. 104-208) was enacted with purposes that provide additional support for access. Its purposes include the promotion of library services that provide all users access to information through state, regional, national, and international electronic networks; the provision of linkages among and between libraries; and the promotion of targeted library services to people of diverse geographic, cultural, and socioeconomic backgrounds, to individuals with disabilities, and to people with limited functional literacy or information skills.[7] The American Library Association, the Chief Officers of State Library Agencies (COSLA), and the Urban Libraries Council worked to develop the LSTA as a replacement for the Library Services and Construction Act and lobbied for its passage in collaboration with ALA's Washington Office. The LSTA was authorized at $150 million for fiscal year 1997 and "such sums" for each year through 2002. Most of the LSTA funds, administered by the Institute of Museum and Library Services (IMLS), were allocated to state library agencies for statewide services or subgrants for technological innovation, electronic linkage, or outreach.[8]

State library agencies have Web sites with five-year plans outlining areas of focus for technology funding as required by IMLS. These Web sites are a rich source for gaining an overview of the extent to which the states have committed to connectivity, access, and fostering technological training.[9] The two broad priorities of LSTA are for activities using technology for information sharing between libraries and other community services and making library programs more accessible to urban, rural, or low-income residents.

Public libraries, viewed by many as a public point of Internet access, are an important component in bridging the digital divide between the wired-information rich and the urban and rural disadvantaged. At the first national Digital Divide Summit sponsored by the Department of Commerce in December 1999, libraries were identified as sustainable access points for providing training.[10] Recognizing that libraries have a heritage of providing free information, the Gates Learning Foundation has awarded grants to 1,300 public libraries in twenty-eight states with a five-year plan to provide grants to 11,000 more public libraries, including training for librarians.[11]

The Technology Opportunities Program (TOP), the new incarnation of the TIIAP program, provides continued support to projects that will demonstrate practical applications of new telecommunications and information technologies to serve the public interest. The project application area "Community Networking and Services" is a good fit for community building as its purposes include (1) funding of community information systems that allow end users to draw upon an expanding variety of information resources, (2) creating online mechanisms for social service delivery, and (3) designing innovative access models for populations whose access has been limited or prevented by geographic barriers, economic distress, linguistic or acculturation problems, age, or distance. The "Lifelong Learning and the Arts" project application area features as examples creative partnerships among schools, libraries, museums, colleges, and universities to deliver network-based learning resources.[12] Awards for the year 2000 have not yet been made, but it is likely that libraries will continue to be prominent in selection for funding under the Technology Opportunities Program as they were under TIIAP.

These resources, coupled with the investments made through LSTA and by state, regional, and local libraries, have positioned public libraries to be an important part of the national effort to provide access to digital information. Most of the work has been accomplished within a decade. This has meant an investment in training and the addition of staff versed in digital technologies.

Using Librarians' Digital Expertise to Build Community

The use of the World Wide Web to enhance access to information has been realized conceptually by the development of "The Community

Connector," an electronic gateway project directed by Joan C. Durrance and Paul Resnick at the University of Michigan School of Information. The project supports community-serving organizations, funders, academics, and students who are using technology to enhance geographic communities.[13]

There are many examples of libraries providing community information on the Web, as described by projects implemented under TIIAP and using funding (in many cases) from the Library Services and Technology Act (LSTA). For instance, Sarasota County Library System in Florida worked with the county's Human Services Planning Association to develop a community information system and a Web site with information and referral (I&R) data and an I&R system that provides access to current multiple agencies. Also in Florida, the St. John's Library System led an effort to compile and disseminate information on available human resources for community residents using the Alliance of Information and Retrieval Services taxonomy and linking to human services agencies' Web sites.[14] A review of Web sites of public libraries throughout the United States shows various initiatives to link users with community information through the library.

Whether libraries and librarians will maintain a strong leadership role in developing and supporting community information networks is an open question. In their book *Civic Space/Cyberspace: The American Public Library in the Information Age,* Redmond Kathleen Molz and Phyllis Dain note,

> But for those civic networks in which there is no public library involvement, their emphasis on local events and activities and their capacity to link themselves to other sources of information, including the Internet, could lead perhaps to an encroachment on or even a displacement of the public library's information and referral (I and R) services, which some librarians believe were among the precursors of community networking.[15]

This concern provided some of the context for Bajjaly's *Community Networking Handbook,* in which he wrote:

> I see considerable untapped potential for community networking initiatives—whether already up-and-running or yet to be started—to benefit from the full participation of the public library. . . . There are about 215 established community networks in the United States and Canada. Less than one third identify a library as a major partner.[16]

Indeed there is support for community networking coming from other disciplines. For example, the Community Information Technology Center, an initiative of the UCLA Advanced Policy Institute at the School of Public Policy and Social Research, assists community organizations in applying new technologies to their work, including Web site design, municipal information systems and information systems design.[17] Also, well-realized virtual communities, such as FortNet— Your Town on the Net, a public service organization dedicated to introducing Internet technologies to northern Colorado citizens, have been developed that include libraries but are not maintained by libraries. [18]

The Viability of Cybercommunity

There is a difference, however, between the creation of access tools and the provision of workstations and support for their use in public libraries. The emergence of cybercommunities has been the topic of interesting discussion and is pertinent to this book's focus on community building, for some seem to think that cybercommunities or virtual communities might displace real communities.

In "The Internet and Political Transformation," Bruce Bimber observes that there are two sorts of claims to large-scale transformations in the structure of political influence caused by the swift development of the Internet: the populist claim that the Internet will erode the influence of organized groups and political elites, and the community-building claim that the Internet will cause a restructuring of the nature of community and the foundations of social order. Bimber suggests that neither will happen and that what we will see is an accelerated pluralism with the Internet contributing to the ongoing fragmentation of interest-based politics with a shift toward a more fluid, issue-based group politics with less institutional coherence.[19]

Musing on this same issue, Amitai and Oren Etzioni ask, "What virtues of online communities are absent in off-line ones?" They conclude that real communities are better than virtual ones in communicating affect, in identifying participants and holding them accountable, and in providing group feedback. Online communities, however, let people bond without being in proximity and can evolve beyond borders and time zones, encompass individuals who are homebound, and accommodate more individuals than a meeting room. In the future, a mixed person–machine system might prevail over pure interpersonal or computer-mediated systems.[20]

These issues are part of the focus of a number of groups, such as the Association for Community Networking (AFCN), an educational nonprofit corporation dedicated to fostering and supporting community-based creation and provision of appropriate technology services. Focuses of AFCN are to help find commonsense, practical ways to use the power of both electronic and personal contact to build healthy communities, and to help each community decide for itself how it wants to use technology.[21]

The Center for Civic Networking provides links to other public information spaces for the twenty-first century, including the Technology Project, a Rockefeller Family Fund project that seeks to accelerate social and political progress by building technological capacity for community collaboration and citizen management.[22] The most fully developed statement that analyzes the technology needs of the nonprofit sector is the blueprint released by the National Strategy for Nonprofit Technology, which recommended a new entity, the Nonprofit Technology Enterprise Network (N-TEN).[23] The library community at local and policy levels is not prominent among the boards that have fostered these projects.[24]

Yet balance must always be considered. Writing of the myth of the virtual community, Joseph Lockard notes, "Emergent cyberspace ideologies commonly promote credence in machine-mediated social relations and their benefits, together with mystifications of individual, community, and global relations. . . . If we embrace cyberspace uncritically without a political consciousness of its structured dreams, then we are certain to awake 'in the tentacles of the octopus.'"[25] The next decade will most likely see a shakeout in the cybercommunity building environment. The role of librarians is yet to be determined, but it may well be that librarians who meld the real and the virtual will keep the octopus at bay.

Librarians: A Keystone Species

"Technology development and use must be mediated by heart," observe Bonnie Nardi and Vicki L. O'Day in their book *Information Ecologies*.[26] They define "keystone species" as those species crucial to the shape and stability of an ecosystem. Librarians are identified as a keystone species with interaction skills, strategic expertise, willingness to evaluate information, and the ability to build relationships.[27]

The role of librarians in the future, states Walt Crawford, is revolution through evolution.[28] Partnerships and interaction with civic networking movements are other facets of community building that librarians can foster as we seek to bring librarian values and commitment to information access into the new century.

ENDNOTES

1. National Telecommunications and Information Administration. Accessed January 1, 2000. Available <*http://www.ntia.doc.gov/*>.

2. Stephen T. Bajjaly, *The Community Networking Handbook* (Chicago: American Library Association, 1999).

3. Ibid., 12.

4. ALA Office for Information and Technology Policy. Accessed January 12, 2000. Available <*http://www.ala.org/oitp/about.html*>. For background on early identification of the profession's need to move into this area, see Kathleen M. Heim, "National Information Policy and a Mandate for Oversight by the Information Professions," *Government Publications Review* 13 (January–February 1986): 21–37.

5. Schools and Libraries Division, Universal Service Administrative Company. Accessed January 2000. Available <*http://www.sl.universalservice.org/*>. See also Education and Libraries Networks Coalition (EdLiNC) at <*http://www.edlinc.org/*>. Accessed January 22, 2000.

6. John Carlo Bertot and Charles R. McClure, *Moving toward More Effective Public Internet Access: The 1998 National Survey of Public Library Outlet Internet Connectivity* (Washington, D.C.: U.S. National Commission on Libraries and Information Science, 1999).

7. "About IMLS: Museum and Library Services Act of 1996." Accessed January 14, 2000. Available <*http://www.imls.gov/about_abt1966.htm*>.

8. "Library Services and Technology Act Enacted," ALA Washington Office. Accessed January 14, 2000. Available <*http://www.ala.org/washoff/lstapass.html*>.

9. "State Library Homepages," Chief Officers of State Library Agencies. Accessed January 14, 2000. Available <*http://www.cosla.org/states.html*>.

10. Digital Divide Network. Accessed January 12, 2000. Available <*http://www.digitaldividenetwork.org*>.

11. "Libraries and Access to Information," Bill and Melinda Gates Foundation. Accessed January 12, 2000. Available <*http://www.glf.org/Libraries/*>.

12. "Top 2000 Notice," U.S. Department of Commerce, National Telecommunications and Information Administration, Technology Opportunities Program. Accessed January 22, 2000. Available *<http://www.ntia.doc.gov/otiahome/tiiap/application/notice2000.html>*.

13. "The Community Connector." Accessed January 12, 2000. Available *<http://www.si.umich.edu/Community/about.html>*.

14. Gloria Colvin, David Hoak, and Nancy Pike, "Linking Community Resources," *Florida Libraries* 42 (September/October 1999): 93–94.

15. Redmond Kathleen Molz and Phyllis Dain, *Civic Space/Cyberspace: The American Public Library in the Information Age* (Cambridge, Mass.: MIT Press, 1999), 171.

16. Bajjaly, *Community Networking Handbook,* ix.

17. Community Information Technology Center. Accessed January 15, 2000. Available *<http://api.sppsp.ucla.edu/serv.htm>*.

18. FortNet: The Community Information Network. Accessed January 15, 2000. Available *<http://www.fortnet.com/>*.

19. Bruce Bimber, "The Internet and Political Transformation: Populism, Community, and Accelerated Pluralism," *Polity* 31 (fall 1998): 133–160.

20. Amitai Etzioni and Oren Etzioni, "Communities: Virtual or Real?" *Science* 277 (July 1997): 295.

21. Association for Community Networking: Background. Accessed January 15, 2000. Available *<http://www.afcn.net/mission.html>*.

22. Center for Civic Networking. Accessed January 15, 2000. Available *<http://www.civicnet.org>*; and Technology Project. Accessed January 15, 2000. Available *<http://www.techproject.org/description.html>*.

23. Nonprofit Technology Enterprise Network. Accessed January 15, 2000. Available *<http://www.nten.org/>*.

24. American Library Association, *Handbook of Organization 1999–2000* (Chicago: American Library Association, 1999), 139. ALA does not list membership in the Association for Community Networking or the Nonprofit Technology Enterprise Network.

25. Joseph Lockard, "Progressive Politics, Electronic Individualism, and the Myth of Virtual Community," in *Internet Culture,* ed. David Porter (New York: Routledge, 1997), 230.

26. Bonnie A. Nardi and Vicki L. O'Day, *Information Ecologies: Using Technology with Heart* (Cambridge, Mass.: MIT Press, 1999), x.

27. Ibid., 79–104.

28. Walt Crawford, *Being Analog: Creating Tomorrow's Libraries* (Chicago: American Library Association, 1999).

7 Closing the Circle

Connecting the Public Library Transformation Process to Community Building

The central concern of this book is to explore what it means to build community and how librarians can participate. Thus far, the many dimensions of community have been discussed as well as the challenge of diversity. The lack of a library presence on the national community building landscape has been established. What it means to build communities comprehensively has been analyzed, and the framework developed at the Wilder Foundation has been used to provide examples. The fact that libraries and their services fit very well into the schema of the national community building model has been demonstrated through use of the Wilder framework and stories of community building librarians from the front lines. Cybercommunities have been examined to gain understanding of the direction in which telecommunications have shifted much energy and resources. What remains is to make a meaningful connection between the work librarians do and the national movement to build community.

Key Areas of Linkage for Community Building and Librarians

Librarians who share the values that drive community building will find insights by considering the areas of focus of comprehensive community initiatives (CCIs). As was shown in chapter 3, CCIs are the current base for community building across systems. By linking the general CCI areas of focus to daily library work life, it is possible to begin to lay the groundwork for ensuring that librarians will be integral to community building. Of course, each community is different and local needs will dictate direction.

The areas of focus discussed in this chapter have been derived from a review of the comprehensive community initiative literature.[1] The CCI literature is not only important for the examples that demonstrate initiatives where community-building-oriented librarians will readily identify their role but as an introduction and resource list to some of the organizations and policy-making entities with which the library community should seek linkage.

Because libraries and librarians have not been included in the databases that identify community building components, actual examples with reference to the literature are provided that demonstrate logical connections. The lack of inclusion of libraries and librarians is not because they do not participate in these kinds of initiatives, but because their participation has not been connected or identified as integral to community building by policy analysts and scholars.

As additional illustration of the philosophical connection between the CCI models and current library practice, reference to the public library transformation process is provided for each area of focus.[2] This will demonstrate that librarians can close the circle. By presenting areas of focus of CCIs, identifying actual library examples, and indicating which "public library service response" from *Planning for Results* fits, the connections will be clear.

Arts and Culture

Arts and culture (in general) as community building activities are not recognized as comprehensive to the degree that might be expected. The Art Works! project, a prevention program for youth at risk sponsored by the National Endowment for the Arts, and the Learning Systems Group's Creative Partnerships for Prevention: Using the Arts and Humanities to Build Resiliency in Youth are two examples of arts- and humanities-related initiatives identified as contributing to community building.[3] Although arts and humanities at least appear as a category in the community building initiative databases (unlike libraries), their presence is a pale reflection of the impact that they could make if they were more broadly represented in policy-making bodies that participate in community building.

Libraries would do well to ally themselves with the arts and the humanities in community building efforts. The *National Connections* project, described briefly in chapter 5 as an example of a community building initiative at the Johnson County (Kansas) Library, is an ideal example of a library-based effort that takes a comprehensive approach to community building.[4] *National Connections* funded forty adult reading–discussion projects in public libraries in 1999. Each project was a collaboration among agencies for adult learners as well as the library and the humanities council. Other library-based reading–discussion programs, such as family literacy, would meet criteria for community building as they seek to enhance the life skills of the at-risk population.

Planning for Results: Cultural Awareness (p. 82); Lifelong Learning (p. 113).

Child and Youth Development

Child development is a major focus of community building initiatives. Examples highlighted as exceptional include the Danforth Foundation–funded project, *Serving Children, Youth and Families through Interprofessional Collaboration and Service Integration,* conducted at Miami University.[5] This project provides models for interprofessional collaboration and service integration designed to meet the needs of children. Another outstanding example is the report of work done on community mobilization by the Families and Work Institute, which includes sections on re-forming communities to serve the families of young children and improving and ensuring quality of services.[6] The interconnectedness of youth problems can be more effectively dealt with through comprehensive community initiatives rather than through treatment of specific behaviors.[7]

The lack of inclusion of libraries and their services in analyses of community building is especially disappointing in light of such current library initiatives as the DeWitt Wallace Reader's Digest Fund project Public Libraries as Partners in Youth Development or the fund's National Library Power project.[8] Both of these national youth-focused library initiatives exemplify the kind of work that librarians do in service of community-based child and youth development. Getting the library story to community builders so that the work of librarians can be viewed as part of comprehensive community initiatives is yet to be accomplished.

Planning for Results (No age-specific responses are listed.): Basic Literacy (p. 58); Information Literacy (p. 108); Lifelong Learning (p. 113).

City Services and Infrastructure

Community builders are beginning to generate an impressive literature examining government services in a system context. The National Research Council study *Governance and Opportunity in Metropolitan America,* examines the geography of economic and social opportunity, social stratification, and fiscal and service disparities within metropolitan areas.[9] In *City Making: Building Community without Building Walls,* Gerald E. Frug describes decentralization of power based on the recognition of the impact that cities within a single metropolitan area have upon each other.[10] Neither study includes library services in the discussion.

Yet this focus—city services and infrastructure—is one area of community building in which libraries and librarians have long led the way. The many examples of effective library cooperation in reciprocal borrowing or technology planning, for instance, are really prototypes of the kinds of services that these infrastructure studies suggest. The collaborative work of libraries in cooperation can position librarians as change leaders in their communities, as has been well described by Bruce E. Daniels in "State Libraries: Architects for the Information Highway."[11]

Planning for Results: Commons (p. 67); Government Information (p. 103).

Community Development

This area of focus concerns efforts to create and maintain positive neighborhood environments, including building or reconstructing housing, social services, and economic development. *Community Development in the 1990s,* a review published by the Urban Institute, used system performance indicators to measure community capacity and identified other aspects of nonphysical development that community development corporations might consider.[12]

Two reports issued by the Brookings Institution in the volume *Urban Problems and Community Development* also provide insight into the community development aspect of comprehensive community initiatives.[13] "Swimming against the Tide: A Brief History of Federal Policy in Poor Communities" emphasizes the need for comprehensive community building, and "What Community Supplies" reviews the social organization of low-income communities.

An excellent library publication that addresses many of the issues surrounding the need for libraries to collaborate in community development is *Poor People and Library Services,* edited by Karen Venturella, which examines ways in which public libraries serve poor people in urban and rural settings.[14]

Planning for Results: Government Information (p. 103); Local History and Genealogy (p. 118).

Economic Development

Economic development as a comprehensive community building issue examines how residents may increase opportunities for jobs and business creation. In "The Competitive Advantage of the Inner City," Michael Porter analyzes the need for community revitalization efforts to focus on the creation of business opportunities.[15] School-to-work programs are seen as essential in Joan Fitzgerald's case study of schools and community-based organizations.[16] Both of these studies provide logical methods by which economic development can take place, but the role that libraries might play is overlooked. Economic development and service to business are areas in which libraries excel.

Norman Walzer's study of the role of rural Illinois public libraries in economic development also demonstrates the strength of libraries in this aspect of community building, while *Helping Business: The Library's Role in Community Economic Development* provides a blueprint for action overall.[17]

Planning for Results: Business and Career Information (p. 62).

Education

School-linked or school-based programs aimed at improving outcomes for youth and families create another opportunity for community development efforts. Elaine Morley and Shelli B. Rossman examined community-based collaboratives that focused on service integration or on comprehensive service delivery that addressed multiple needs by implementing a broad-based continuum of care.[18] The collaboratives the authors examined included SafeFutures, Communities in Schools, New Futures, Children at Risk, and the Comprehensive Communities Program. The Communities in Schools program model—with more than one hundred sites nationwide—is based on using existing community resources and services. These vary by community but could include counseling, tutoring, pregnancy prevention, and teaching study skills.

Support for community school collaboration initiatives has been especially strong from the National Center for Community Education, which provides leadership training to those interested in community schools and which has been engaged to provide training to schools awarded grants as Twenty-first Century Community Learning Centers (CCLC). The Twenty-first CCLC program is a key component of the U.S. Department of Education, funded at $450 million in fiscal year 2000. Although collaboration with other community public and nonprofit organizations is a strong feature of the Twenty-first CCLC initiative, public libraries are not emphasized in news coverage or abstracts of the grants awarded.[19]

An expanded role for public libraries in nonschool youth development is being supported by the Public Libraries as Partners in Youth Development initiative mentioned earlier in the section "Child and Youth Development." With substantive support from the DeWitt Wallace Reader's Digest Fund, demonstration grants should provide public libraries an opportunity to take their place in comprehensive community initiatives.

Planning for Results: Basic Literacy (p. 58); Current Topics and Titles (p. 87); Formal Learning Support (p. 92); Lifelong Learning (p. 113).

Employment/Workforce

Meaningful jobs and employment programs grew as a focus for CCIs in the late 1990s in large part because of welfare reform as enacted in the Personal Responsibility and Work Opportunity Reconciliation Act of 1996. The Center for Community Change (CCC) provides assistance for organizations that work in low-income communities, works to give low-income people a voice in public policies, leads campaigns to make foundations and funders aware of and responsive to low-income communities, conducts studies, and sponsors projects. *Strengthening Rural Economies: Programs That Target Promising Sectors of a Local Economy,* published by the CCC for the Office of Policy Development and Research of the U.S. Department of Housing and Urban Development, focuses on rural sector jobs and job creation.[20] Another publication of the CCC, *Making Connections: A Study of Employment Linkage Programs,* includes analysis of job information support structures.[21]

At the 1999 ALA Annual Conference, in the Reference and User Services Association's Business Reference and Services Section program, Edgar McCray, Jobs and Careers Librarian in the Business and Technology Department of the San Francisco Public Library, provided an outstanding program on the role public libraries play in providing career assistance.[22]

Also, Joan C. Durrance, in *Meeting Community Needs with Job and Career Services,* provides information on how libraries can assist communities in job and career development. [23]

Planning for Results: Business and Career Information (p. 62).

Faith-based Development

Much recent community development has occurred in cooperation with faith-based organizations. This collaboration has grown since the Personal Responsibility and Work Opportunity Reconciliation Act of 1996 was passed. The act included a "charitable choice" provision permitting contracts, vouchers, and other funding to allow charitable, religious, or private organizations to provide services under the Temporary Assistance for Needy Families (TANF), Medicaid, Supplemental Security Income, and Food Stamp programs. Charitable choice has highlighted how state and local agencies can involve congregations and faith-based organizations in welfare reform. This development has been well summarized by Jessica Yates in a paper published by the Welfare Information Network.[24]

Libraries have been included along with faith-based organizations among those entities that provide and fund extralearning activities by the National Governors' Association as part of its "Smartkids4our-Future: Preparing Kids for Success" program.[25] Libraries have also been linked with faith-based organizations by the Ohio Literacy Initiative, which fosters community partnerships in literacy and family literacy.[26]

Planning for Results: Library involvement would be a factor of the projects assumed by the faith-based organizations.

Family Services

In response to the needs of families, holistic services that provide support for the entire unit are well suited to the comprehensive community approach. The Family Resource Coalition of America (FRCA) (Family Support America as of 5/1/00) is an alliance of people and organizations that work to strengthen America's families. FRCA's best practices project identified critical areas for comprehensive community support.[27] The National Network for Family Resiliency, part of the Children, Youth, and Families at Risk Network, supports families facing multiple tasks through land-grant universities in collaboration with Cooperative State Research, the National 4-H Council, and Cooperative Extension.[28]

Literacy is one of the key challenges under the family services focus area for public libraries. In her book, *Community Collaborations for Family Literacy Handbook,* S. Shelley Quezada examines public library programs that develop family literacy in the context of community.[29] The Fact Sheet series issued by the American Library Association provides an overview of family literacy partnerships that help communities become more productive and literate, including the Bell-Atlantic–ALA Family Literacy Project and the Cargill Cares project.[30]

Planning for Results: Basic Literacy (p. 58); Community Referral (p. 72).

Health

Health care for vulnerable and underserved populations is increasingly being considered as an aspect of comprehensive community initiatives. An example of work that looks at health care from this perspective is that done by the Coalition for Healthier Cities and Communities, which stimulates and encourages collaborative action and efficient use of resources from multiple sectors and community systems.[31] The idea of communities working together for health care has been explored in *Collaborating to Improve Community Health,* which shows how key players from local governments, schools, churches, and health care organizations can work together to improve communities.[32]

Although libraries are seldom mentioned in the literature of comprehensive community initiatives, one example of a public library working in this context is the Aurora, Illinois, public library, which participates in THINK, the teen health information network, a partnership of public libraries, schools, and community agencies.[33]

Planning for Results: Community Referral (p. 72); Consumer Information (p. 77); General Information (p. 98).

Housing

Housing has been the rallying point for much community building work. The community development movement initially organized around the creation and rehabilitation of housing with community building components added later. Walker and Weinheimer's study of community development corporations (CDCs) in twenty-three cities notes that since 1991, more than 90,000 units have been added.[34] Funding has been spearheaded by the Local Initiatives Support Corporation, which acts as an intermediary for more than nine hundred corporations and foundations. The corporation provides technical support and financial resources to help CDCs become strong and stable neighborhood institutions characterized by effective and responsible fiscal management and capable of carrying out a wide range of revitalization activities.[35] Connection of housing to community building has been examined in the *Journal of Housing and Community Development,* published by the National Association of Housing and Redevelopment Officials.

Library connection to housing has been discussed in several case studies of service provided in public housing facilities.[36] The opportunity for library involvement in community development in housing initiatives is great.

Planning for Results: Community Referral (p. 72); Consumer Information (p. 77); Government Information (p. 103).

Welfare and Income Support

The welfare reform legislation of the 1990s refocused the work of comprehensive community initiatives. *Programs in Aid of the Poor* analyzes the broad changes in federal assistance and the results of the 1996 welfare reform.[37] The asset approach to building community has been presented in *Building the Bridge from Client to Citizen: A Community Toolbox for Welfare Reform,* which focuses on associational support for community building activities.[38]

Many library programs could fit into community building initiatives based upon welfare reform. The profession's philosophical policy statement on these issues is "Library Services for the Poor," which notes that "it is crucial that libraries recognize their role in enabling poor people to participate fully in a democratic society, by utilizing a wide variety of available resources and strategies. Concrete programs of training and development are needed to sensitize and prepare library staff to identify poor people's needs and deliver relevant services."[39] Additional resources for working with poor people are presented on the Web page of the Hunger, Homelessness and Poverty Task Force of the Social Responsibilities Roundtable of the American Library Association.[40]

Planning for Results: Community Referral (p. 72); Consumer Information (p. 77); Government Information (p. 103).

Other Areas of Comprehensive Community Building

The Community Building Resource Exchange also includes the environment, public safety, and substance abuse as areas in which comprehensive community initiatives can coalesce. Library responses to these areas as identified in *Planning for Results* include Community Referral (p. 72); Consumer Information (p. 77); Current Topics and Titles (p. 87); and General Information (p. 98).

This review has been complex. The term *community building* is used interchangeably for overall effort and for more specific work that converges on structure. Our look at areas of focus is neither prescriptive nor comprehensive. It is based on major substantive concerns selected as a framing device for examining librarians and community building because it consolidates work from many areas that coincide with librarians' values.

The goal has been to demonstrate that the areas of focus of community building have salience for the work of librarians. In fact, librarians in daily practice develop and deliver programs that fit into the comprehensive community initiative model. The public library profession's current planning document, *Planning for Results: A Public Library Transformation Process,* identifies public library responses that articulate with the concerns of CCIs.

ENDNOTES

1. "The Aspen Institute Roundtable on CCIs," Community Building Resource Exchange. Accessed January 6, 2000. Available *<http://www.commbuild.org/index.html>*. A search of the site finds no mention of the contributions of libraries.

2. Ethel Himmel and William James Wilson, *Planning for Results: A Public Library Transformation Process* (Chicago: American Library Association, 1998).

3. "Art Works! Prevention Programs for Youth and Communities," National Endowment for the Arts; hard copy from National Clearinghouse for Alcohol and Drug Information, 1997. Accessed January 6, 2000. Available *<http://www.health.org/artworks/index.htm>*; and "Creative Partnerships for Prevention: Using the Arts and Humanities to Build Resiliency in Youth," Learning Systems Group. Accessed January 6, 2000. Available *<http:// www.cpprev.org/contents.htm>*.

4. American Library Association, Office of Public Programs. Accessed January 6, 2000. Available *<http://www.ala.org/publicprograms/national/general.html>*.

5. Katharine Briar, *Serving Children, Youth and Families through Interprofessional Collaboration and Service Integration* (Oxford, Ohio: The Danforth Foundation and the Institute for Educational Renewal at Miami University, 1994).

6. *Community Mobilization: Strategies to Support Young Children and Their Families* (New York: Families and Work Institute, 1996).

7. William H. Barton, Marie Watkinds, and Roger Jarjoura, "Youth and Communities: Toward Comprehensive Strategies for Youth Development," in *Community Building: Renewal, Well-Being, and Shared Responsibility,* ed. Patricia Ewalt, Edith M. Freeman, and Dennis L. Poole (Washington, D.C.: NASW Press, 1998).

8. "Public Libraries as Partners in Youth Development, an Initiative of the DeWitt Wallace Reader's Digest Fund" (1999 ongoing). Accessed January 6, 2000. Available *<http://www.ala.org/plpyd/dwtoc.html>*; and Douglas L. Zweizig et al., *Lessons from Library Power: Enriching Teaching and*

Learning: Final Report of the Evaluation of the National Library Power Initiative, an Initiative of the DeWitt Wallace Reader's Digest Fund (Littleton, Colo.: Libraries Unlimited, 1999).

9. Committee on Improving the Future of U.S. Cities through Improved Metropolitan Area Governance, *Governance and Opportunity in Metropolitan America* (Washington, D.C.: National Academy Press, 1999).

10. Gerald E. Frug, *City Making: Building Community without Building Walls* (Princeton, N.J.: Princeton University Press, 1999).

11. Bruce E. Daniels, "State Libraries: Architects for the Information Highway," *Bottom Line* 9, no. 1 (1996): 6–9.

12. Christopher Walker and Mark Weinheimer, *Community Development in the 1990s* (Washington, D.C.: The Urban Institute, 1998).

13. Ronald F. Ferguson and William T. Dickens, eds., *Urban Problems and Community Development* (Washington, D.C.: Brookings Institution, 1998), includes Alice O'Connor, "Swimming against the Tide: A Brief History of Federal Policy in Poor Communities," and Robert J. Sampson, "What Community Supplies."

14. Karen M. Venturella, *Poor People and Library Services,* with a foreword by Sanford Berman (Jefferson, N.C.: McFarland, 1998).

15. Michael Porter, "The Competitive Advantage of the Inner City," *Harvard Business Review* 73 (May–June 1995): 55–71.

16. Joan Fitzgerald, "Linking School-to-Work Programs to Community Economic Development in Urban Schools," *Urban Education* 32 (November 1997): 489–511.

17. Norman Walzer, "Rural Public Libraries and Community Economic Development," *Illinois Libraries* 79 (fall 1997): 178–181; and Maxine Bleiweis, *Helping Business: The Library's Role in Community Economic Development* (New York: Neal-Schuman, 1997).

18. Elaine Morley and Shelli B. Rossman, *Helping Youth-at-Risk: Lessons from Community-based Initiatives* (Washington, D.C.: The Urban Institute, 1997).

19. National Center for Community Education. Accessed January 22, 2000. Available <*http://www.nccenet.org/the_center/index.htm*>; Twenty-first Century Community Learning Centers, Program Notices. Accessed January 22, 2000. Available <*http://www.ed.gov/21stcclc/*>.

20. Alan Okagaki, Chris Palmer, and Neil S. Mayer, *Strengthening Rural Economies: Programs That Target Promising Sectors of a Local Economy* (Washington, D.C.: Center for Community Change, December 1998).

21. Frieda Molina, *Making Connections: A Study of Employment Linkage Programs* (Washington, D.C.: Center for Community Change, May 1998).

22. See the Jobs and Careers Center page of the San Francisco Public Library. Accessed January 6, 2000. Available *<http://206.14.7.53/btdir/careers.html>*.

23. Joan C. Durrance, *Meeting Community Needs with Job and Career Services* (New York: Neal-Schuman, 1994).

24. Jessica Yates, "Partnerships with the Faith Community in Welfare Reform," Welfare Information Network, Issue Notes series. Accessed January 9, 2000. Available *<http://www.wlfareinfo.org/faith.htm>*. The Welfare Information Network, a clearinghouse for information, policy analysis, and technical assistance on welfare reform, is a special activity of the Finance Project, a national initiative to create knowledge and share information that will lead to the improved well-being of families, children, and communities. Accessed January 9, 2000. Available *<http://www.financeproject.org>*.

25. The inclusion of libraries and faith-based organizations as extra-learning opportunities demonstrates an area for collaboration.

26. Ohio Literacy Initiative, "Community Support." Accessed January 9, 2000. Available *<http://www.ode.state.oh.us/Lit_init/Community.htm>*.

27. Family Resource Coalition of America. Accessed January 6, 2000. Available *<http://www.frca.org>*.

28. National Network for Family Resiliency, "Building Family Strengths to Meet Life's Challenges." Accessed January 6, 2000. Available *<http://www.nnfr.org/about.html>*.

29. S. Shelley Quezada, *Community Collaborations for Family Literacy Handbook* (New York: Neal-Schuman, 1993).

30. "Family Literacy—Helping Parents Help Their Children," ALA Fact Sheet, April 1999, American Library Association. Accessed January 11, 2000. Available *<http://www.ala.org/pio/factsheets/familyliteracy.html>*.

31. This coalition works in the context of community building and health care provision. Accessed January 9, 2000. Available *<http://www.healthycommunities.org>*.

32. Kathryn Johnson, Wynne Grossman, and Anne Cassidy, *Collaborating to Improve Community Health: Workbook and Guide to Best Practices in Creating Healthier Communities and Populations* (San Francisco: Jossey-Bass, 1997).

33. Judith Kuzel and S. Erickson, "The Teen Health Information Network," *Illinois Libraries* 77 (fall 1995): 157.

34. Walker and Weinheimer, *Community Development in the 1990s*, 1.

35. Local Initiatives Support Corporation. Accessed January 9, 2000. Available *<http://www.liscnet.org>*.

36. See, for example, Mary D. Teasley and Deloris Walker-Moses, "On-site Centers at Public Housing Sites," in *Poor People and Library Services,* ed. Venturella; Candice Brown, "A Library District Reaches Out: Serving the African American Community in a Public Housing Complex," *Colorado Libraries* 21 (summer 1995): 30–31; and Susan Herring, "Peoria Public Library and the Peoria Housing Authority Celebrate Twenty-five Years of Cooperation," *Illinois Libraries* 75 (fall 1993): 315–317.

37. Sar A. Levitan, *Programs in Aid of the Poor,* 7th ed., revised and updated by Garth L. Magnum and Stephen L. Magnum (Baltimore: Johns Hopkins University Press, 1998).

38. John P. Kretzmann and Michael B. Green, *Building the Bridge from Client to Citizen: A Community Toolbox for Welfare Reform* (Evanston, Ill.: Institute for Policy Research, 1998); also published in *Shelterforce,* no. 96 (November–December 1997).

39. "Library Services for the Poor," in the *ALA Policy Manual* as it appears in the *ALA Handbook of Organization 1999–2000* (Chicago: American Library Association, 1999), 49–50.

40. SRRT Hunger, Homelessness and Poverty Task Force of the American Library Association. Accessed January 10, 2000. Available *<http://libr. org/HHP/>*.

8 New Models of Work
A Librarian at Every Table

This chapter is based on the assumption that community building must be a goal of U.S. public libraries. Every library will have its own vision statement that describes a future ideal condition.[1] Although some libraries may not choose community building as a goal, if community building is part of the community's vision, not doing so might make the library irrelevant.[2] Earlier chapters have described how community building has come to be a value of communities in the United States. Federal, state, and local governments as well as numerous foundations have used the community building model as a condition for funding comprehensive community initiatives. The advent of cybercommunities has expanded the community building concept, and focus on the digital divide has extended community building interest through LSTA and TOPS funding.[3]

The 1999–2000 presidential theme of Sarah Ann Long as presented in her speech to the Communitarian Summit in February 1999 affirms that libraries can make a substantial contribution to community building. In support of strengthening community, Long makes these observations about the public library:

- The public library has a historical role in civic education.
- The public library is open to people of all ages, races, and economic levels.
- It is a public meeting place for groups and individuals.

- It is a repository of the community's history and culture.
- The public library enjoys popularity and a long tradition of service.
- The public library is staffed by highly educated people.
- The public library extends service to the homebound and others with disabilities.
- The public library has demonstrated leadership in providing access to new technologies.
- The public library is convenient, with central locations in 16,000 sites nationwide.[4]

Long identifies the historical role of the library in helping to create community identity, community dialogue, and community collaboration and also observes that "we can do much more."[5]

Various documents of the American Library Association emphasize this challenge to do more and address aspects of community building[6]:

Priority for Public Awareness, Goal 3: "Libraries are recognized as proactive agencies essential to the cultural, educational, and economic life of society."

Priority for Library Services, Development and Technology, Goal 6: "ALA encourages cooperative activities to improve services to library users," and Goal 11: "Libraries are proactive agencies which meet the challenges of social, economic, and environmental change."

"Position and Public Policy Statements" also affirm community building[7]:

"Libraries: An American Value" includes this principle: "We value our nation's diversity and strive to reflect that diversity by providing a full spectrum of resources and services to the communities we serve."

Policies on minority concerns include, "Goals for Indian Library and Information Services," "Library Education to Meet the Needs of Spanish-Speaking People," and "Library and Information Services to Asian Americans."

Concern for poor people is identified in the association's policy "Library Services for the Poor," which states that "libraries recognize their role in enabling poor people to participate fully in a democratic society," and in *Guidelines for Establishing Community Information and Referral Services in Public Libraries,* which activates the process of linking an individual with a need to a service or a source of information or advice that can fill that need.[8]

The needs of other special populations—the aging, blind, and physically handicapped, those in correctional facilities, the deaf, the institutionalized, and those requiring multilingual materials—are delineated in various standards and guidelines of the association.[9]

Taken together, these priorities, goals, policies, statements, standards, and guidelines combine to frame a commitment to community building on the part of the library profession. Each of these demonstrates a value for librarianship that could find a place as a component of the larger network of initiatives and projects seeking to build community in the United States today. This book has explored the broadest meanings of community building and the lack of inclusion of the work that librarians do in most of the writings and policies about community building.

This is a puzzling situation. Earlier chapters have demonstrated examples of actual and hypothetical library work and actions that meet the criteria of comprehensive community initiative work to strengthen communities. Much of the work that librarians do would, by any definition, be counted as substantive community building activity.

The challenge is for librarians to establish their work and the work of their libraries as contributory to the national movement to build communities comprehensively. Once achieved, the recognition of librarians' roles in community building will make it possible for more partnerships to be formed and more communities strengthened. As previously noted, this is not to say that there are not countless examples of librarians who work to build community. There are. However, their stories are told in outlets that do not reach policy makers. There are very few recent books found in library databases under the subject heading "Libraries and Community," very few abstracts of articles in social science databases that include libraries among community building partners, very few mentions of libraries on the Web sites of community building organizations or in the indexes of reports and books about community building distributed by policy institutes.

The solution is simple but also difficult. A new model of work is needed.

Librarians, library administrators, and librarians in leadership positions must restructure job descriptions and daily work with a community building orientation. This is quite possible. During the 1990s, the work of librarians changed at an accelerated pace because of the broad adoption of the Internet and the World Wide Web and the placement of workstations for public use in public libraries. This change has been accommodated in public libraries with redeployment of resources for staff, equipment, and telecommunication costs. Grants have been obtained, entire new departments focusing on information systems and virtual libraries have been created, and new positions such as Web designer have been added.

Community building is just as important as the integration of new technology. In fact, community building is the foundation for the deployment of resources to new technologies, if this deployment is to be successful. As has been shown in the chapter on building cybercommunities, the need for librarians to participate in the creation of community information network initiatives is as vital as the need to participate in other community activities. Without this participation, the work of librarians will not be perceived as essential.

The Work of Frontline Librarians

Frontline librarians meet the public. Among other responsibilities, they answer reference questions, plan and deliver story hours, conduct readers' advisory services, foster lifelong learning, support users searching the Internet and electronic tools, select library materials, maintain access services, organize collections, plan cultural programs, mount exhibits, prepare publicity, and oversee physical facilities. Their hours are filled with frontline service. In libraries with some travel resources, frontline librarians may attend a state or national library conference or at least a staff development day. They are stretched; they are busy. To add to their workload, ever-newer technologies require intensive staff training and development as upgraded electronic resources or protocols are installed and implemented.

How Does Community Building Fit?

Community building fits because it is fundamental to the survival of the library. Chapter 6 summarized the growth of cybercommunities, but ended with a researcher's observation that "librarians are a keystone species." The observation, though not so articulated, was grounded in the ability of the librarians studied to know their community and their efforts to build it. Without the heart put into daily work that connects people with information and opportunities for lifelong learning assisted by a librarian, users might as well be cut loose to navigate on their own.

Returning to the "Values of Librarians Who Build Community" derived from an analysis of the case studies presented in chapter 5, an outline can be deduced. By incorporating these values into job descriptions and providing support for these values, a new model of work can be crafted.

Community Involvement

Librarians who build community must be involved in the community. This means attending civic association meetings, community development corporation meetings, civic networking meetings, comprehensive community collaborative meetings, visioning focus group meetings, town meetings, or neighborhood council meetings. Comprehensive community initiatives take many forms. The librarian who wants to be a community builder must have an astute sense of the community's direction and must be a full participant in plans to achieve its goals. To do this, if it is a value of the library, time should be provided to attend meetings, and the library must provide coverage of daily responsibilities. This is an investment in the community's resilience and stability. The librarian should participate as a community member first and as a librarian second. In time, as trust is built, the roles will flow together. Consideration should be given to stabilizing communities by keeping successful staff in place.

Awareness of Community Issues

Each community has overarching concerns. These may be the need for economic development, social services, culture, or environmental oversight. For small neighborhood libraries, it is as crucial to read the local weekly paper as it is to read the *New York Times* or the nearest metropolitan daily. Recognition of issues of importance to the community requires concerted interaction with community groups, perhaps as a repository of minutes or records as part of a local history initiative. Because most public librarians are government employees, they may be initially perceived by the public as part of the government bureaucracy and without a stake in the local community. The librarian's demonstration of awareness about current community issues obviates this perception.

Connection as a Responsibility

Librarians who build community will see joining and participating in community associations as a responsibility that will, in the end, lead to greater library use and support. If attendance at community events is perceived as a burden, the goal of community building will not be met. Librarians who attend community events with an open mind and heart will be overwhelmed with opportunities to connect individuals as well as associations in urgent need of information to resources that can be found at the library.

Although the Community Tool Box identifies the library as a passive source of information or meeting room space, connected librarians will be assertive providers of information as it is needed because they will be present at the time of need. Edwin Beckerman has noted that though library staffs might seem to have limited political influence, in smaller and medium-sized libraries where people have more contact with one another, a member of the staff can sometimes reach decision makers more easily than a director can.[10]

Integration of Service

Service integration emerged as a challenge to human services providers during the 1990s. Defined as the process by which a range of educational, health, and social services are delivered in a coordinated way to improve outcomes for individuals and families, service integration strives to overcome the fragmented structure of programs and providers promulgated by professional specializations.[11] Recent attention has focused on the workforce development system, a one-stop, user-friendly center for job seekers and employers, supported by the Workforce Investment Act. The system restructures and streamlines multiple funding sources for scores of programs that aim to provide employment and training assistance to various segments of the population, particularly the economically disadvantaged.[12]

The move to service integration affects all agencies that work in the community. Agencies are expected to be accessible, accountable, affordable, competent, comprehensive, coordinated, ethical, and systemically communicative. Librarians working with human services organizations will demonstrate an ability to span boundaries and provide access to information that is needed regardless of provenance.

Community Building as a Value

Librarians who are community builders see community building as a positive value. They have an intuitive understanding that opening the door every day is not enough. They recognize that they can play a vital role in providing the neighborhood in which they work with a stabilizing influence and that this influence can extend outward to provide resources and information to community organizations. Librarians' internalization of this value compels them to be interested in matters of civic renewal, lifelong learning, and interaction with active residents working to develop a resilient community. These librarians will participate in partnerships and public meetings that are intended to provide stronger neighborhood capacity.

The Library Can Make a Difference

Librarians who build community have an attitude that is positive about the contributions they and their library can make to the community. They attend community activities aware that they bring a skill set that enables them to assist in solving problems. They find ways that the library can be involved in comprehensive community initiatives. If extending learning is deemed a solution to engage youth in after-school programs, the library will be offered as an ideal location.[13] Librarians must be given the power to activate their ideals and to take a place at every table where community building occurs. When authorized to do so, the inherent energy and commitment librarians possess will be freed to build the communities their neighborhoods deserve.

The Role of Library Administrators

Directors of libraries have been successful in building partnerships. Programs and collaborations demonstrate to the community that the library is a viable component in the life of a city, suburb, or small town.

But directors are often so busy with political and governmental responsibilities that day-to-day tending of the neighborhoods and individual communities that make up the library's service area is not possible. Instead, the director should deploy every librarian on staff to help build community. If this were done, the goals of comprehensive community initiatives could be realized. Activating community building requires five steps on the part of library administrators.

1. *Recognize that commitment to build community must be all encompassing.* The decision to foster community building must be as compelling as the decisions made during the 1990s to develop and support connectivity and Internet access. The model of a concerted effort to engage in staff development and training to implement new technologies has been realized. It is a model that can be used to support community building as a public library value. To implement community building as a value will require commitment of staff and resources that parallel the new technologies model.

2. *Authorize and encourage staff to help build community.* If community building is identified as a library goal, staff education and development must be implemented. As with adopting new technologies, some librarians are naturals, while others need both education and support. Once established as a goal, community building should be encouraged by integrating it into the performance review process. Just as librarians might be judged outstanding for their ability to provide user assistance on workstations, so should they be judged outstanding for demonstrating that they have become involved in specific community activities.

3. *Implement personnel policies to help support community building.* To participate in community building activities, the librarian must leave the library (unless the library's meeting room happens to be the location of the meeting). Meaningful involvement requires evening meetings and weekends. In distressed communities, especially, residents must hold community meetings at times outside the conventional workday because they do not have jobs that allow participation during regular business hours. One obstacle to the full acceptance of government employees in community building efforts is the perception that government employees will work for community development on work time only. The classic "insider-outsider" tension identified as a barrier to comprehensive community initiative success must be considered. Community residents who work in the private sector do not receive time or

recognition from their employers for their involvement in community activities. Thus government employees, like librarians, who wish to be an integral part of community building initiatives must be willing to commit to participation during nonwork hours.

For the library administrator to activate a community building outlook, a personnel policy would need to be implemented that would provide a reliable system of substitute librarians and some sort of compensation for hours put in at irregular times. This should be flexible. If a community is undergoing a visioning process, there may be an intense period of community activity requiring a review and adjustment of the librarian's schedule to accommodate full participation.

Throughout the nation public libraries have been the beneficiaries of funding for Gates Labs. Support for these labs has included staff training and development off-site. Once installed, the Gates Labs compel a different type of work structure. The physical presence of new computers is, of course, a tangible entity. Community building is initially intangible and not as seductive as new computers. Yet community building is a national value that is the hope of the new century. If community building is identified as a library value, reorganization of work—using the deployment model implemented to integrate computer technologies—must take place.

4. *Understand that stability is a component of community building.* Large organizations—especially governmental bureaucracies, like library systems—reward excellent performance with promotion to positions that require more supervisory responsibilities and oversight. Bigger is better.

Thus librarians who work to establish credibility and acceptance in a given community may find that their careers can be limited by staying in one place. Yet the very core of community building is the need for stability and continuity. Just as citizens have implored school districts for neighborhood schools, so they would implore library directors for neighborhood libraries staffed by librarians they perceive as vital to the community. Frequent rotation of library personnel from neighborhoods dilutes the effect of community building on the part of the library. If community building commitment is variable among frontline staff, efforts made by an involved librarian might disappear upon reassignment. Unless community building is a part of the organizational culture of a library, gains will not be consolidated.

Without some stability of staff, especially in distressed communities, community building becomes degraded. A parallel example might be the community policing movement. In a rural county, the sheriff's department instituted a program to involve residents in community policing. A neighborhood council was set up and community participation was excellent thanks to an enthusiastic young policewoman who worked hard to recognize and help resolve the community's concerns regarding public safety. After a year of involvement, she was promoted and replaced by a series of officers who had to "get their tickets punched" in community policing to qualify for promotion. The neighborhood council became less enthusiastic and eventually stopped supporting the initiative. Two years later, community residents did not even know who their latest community police officer was—they felt used by the county and realized their community was seen as a pit stop on the road to promotion for individuals and nothing more.

Providing stability to neighborhood libraries requires rethinking total personnel structures. Just as excellent teachers can improve their salaries only through promotion to administration, so it is with most large library systems. Alternative mechanisms of compensation and reward must be developed if excellent librarians are to remain in communities and participate in a meaningful way in community building initiatives. In earlier chapters it has been demonstrated that realization of community is undercut by transient populations, especially in suburbs and edge cities. This holds true for key government employees as well. Principals, teachers, librarians, social services providers can only be effective in their communities if they are given time to get to know and gain the trust of community residents. Lack of administrative attention to stability as a key factor in community building will similarly undercut the efforts of the library to play a role.

5. *Provide resources that affirm community building.* Once a library staff has been encouraged to develop a commitment to community building, the necessary resources must be organized to assist in realization. Thus, if a librarian identifies extended learning as the direction in which a community is moving in trying to provide alternatives for youth at risk, then support to develop such a program needs to be forthcoming from the library system or the librarian must be creative in seeking funding to provide services that articulate with this community goal. This is simply an extension of ideas promoted in the profession's planning tools, but it is the final essential step required of library

administrators who acknowledge that community building is an essential value for their library.

It is the administrators of our nation's libraries who will make it possible for a librarian to be at every table.

The Role of Leadership
in Building Community

Librarianship in the United States has been fortunate to have developed a structure of leadership at the state and national levels that works collaboratively within associations to provide opportunity for policy input to government.[14] These leaders have been essential in achieving successful state and national funding for library support, including the LSCA, LSTA, NCLIS, and Universal Service. They have been successful in mounting national and statewide campaigns that place librarians and libraries high among valued public services. They have worked to connect the library community to funders, including the Gates Foundation, Kellogg, Bell-Atlantic, and DeWitt Wallace. Through established units at the American Library Association (ALA), such as the Office for Information Technology Policy, the Office for Intellectual Freedom, and the Washington Office, working in concert with volunteer advisory committees to each office as well as legislative committees, librarianship has been well represented in many crucial state and national initiatives. Community building requires this level of commitment as well.

Examining the organizational structure of ALA over time reveals patterns of action. As key national issues emerge, the profession appoints committees, develops position and policy papers, and perhaps focuses on these issues as a presidential theme. The next step is the decision to fund a response to the issues with ongoing staff and a volunteer advisory committee. Without this level of commitment, issues float. A good way to ascertain this pattern is to review the list of various memberships maintained by the association.[15] Some of the memberships are simply listed, indicating that ALA sends dues but has no formal liaison (Center for the Study of Responsive Law, Librarians for Nuclear Arms Control, The Progressive, Women in Communications). Others are listed with liaisons (Coalition on Government Information, National Coalition for Literacy, National Forum for Information Literacy). The association's level of commitment to each of the areas of focus of these organizations is a function of a rotating liaison's energy and ability to bring back concerns to the association at large. Because the leadership is elected from a diverse membership, concerns that galvanize one year's elected leaders may not be as central to the next. Except for broad overarching issues, such as intellectual freedom and, more recently, information technology, commitment ebbs and flows. The only way to ensure that a key issue becomes a sustained focus for association concern and resources is to establish an ongoing association unit with a staff and a membership advisory function.

This book has assessed the centrality of community building as a national movement. Community building is the goal of projects supported by many federal agencies, including HUD, the Department of Commerce, the Department of Education, the USDA, and the President's Council on Sustainable Development. Community building is the new nexus for comprehensive community initiatives funded by dozens of foundations and the focus of study of policy institutes and think tanks. Taken together, this concentration of national concern indicates that community building is a movement that has become the focus of national policy formation.

The library profession needs to be at the table of community builders if librarians are to be included and recognized as community builders. There needs to be strong library representation in such groups as the National Community Building Network, the Community Development Society, the Family Resource Coalition (renamed Family Support America in May 2000), the Electronic Policy Network, or the National Community Education Association. The work of librarians needs to be visible in the policy papers and plans for action of the Center for Community Change, the Program on Human and Community Development (John D. and Catherine T. MacArthur Foundation), the Civic Practices Network, Redefining Progress, or the Trillium Foundation.

The way to ensure an ongoing librarian presence among community builders is to establish an office within the American Library Association with responsibility for oversight of national community building initiatives. This office would ensure that the work librarians do becomes part of the agenda and planning process of these initiatives. It would demonstrate that the skills of librarians would solve many of the problems community builders face in identifying information, organizing documentation, or defining a central location for meeting and discussion. In the larger framework, librarians would be clearly at the table, providing solutions to strengthen communities.

The Three-Part Solution

Ensuring that librarianship is a central part of community building requires (1) a restructuring of the work of frontline librarians, (2) the administrative commitment to active participation of librarians in community initiatives, and (3) the efforts of national leadership to secure librarians a full partnership in policy implementation.

These actions are not impossible. The shift of the 1990s to accommodate technology followed this same three-part solution: (1) work was restructured to require and accommodate technological skills, (2) administrative commitment reallocated staff and capital resources, and (3) leadership established an Office for Information Technology Policy within the ALA and identified technology partnerships.

New models of work to accommodate community building would incorporate values the profession has long held. The principles and tenets of community building are embedded in the policy statements of the profession. What remains to be done is to recognize these components in light of the nation's overarching attention to community building and an emphasis that connects these components to local, state, and national initiatives.

ENDNOTES

1. Ethel Himmel and William James Wilson, *Planning for Results: A Public Library Transformation Process* (Chicago: American Library Association, 1998), 25.

2. Ibid.

3. See chapter 6, "Cybercommunity Building and Librarians," for citations to LSTA and TOPS funding for community building projects.

4. Sarah Ann Long, "Libraries Build Communities" (speech presented at the Communitarian Summit, February 1999). Accessed January 11, 2000. Available *<http://www.sarahlong.org/Speeches.speech.htm>*.

5. Ibid.

6. American Library Association, *ALA Policy Manual* (Chicago: ALA, 1999), 29, 30.

7. Ibid., 45, 48–49.

8. Ibid., 49–50; and *Guidelines for Establishing Community Information and Referral Services in Public Libraries,* ed. Norman L. Maas and Dick Manikowski (Chicago: American Library Association, Public Library Association, 1997).

9. "Standards and Guidelines" as listed on the Web page of the American Library Association. Accessed January 11, 2000. Available *<http://www. ala.org/work/standards.html>*.

10. Edwin Beckerman, *Politics and the American Public Library: Creating Political Support for Library Goals* (Lanham, Md.: Scarecrow Press, 1996), 143.

11. National Center for Service Integration. Accessed January 15, 2000. Available *<http://www.cssp.org/kd36.htm>*.

12. Karin Martinson, "Literature Review on Service Coordination and Integration in the Welfare and Workfare Development Systems" (The Urban Institute, January 1999). Accessed January 15, 2000. Available *<http://www.urban.org/welfare/lit_review.html>*.

13. U.S. Department of Education and U.S. Department of Justice, *Safe and Smart: Making After-School Hours Work for Kids* (Washington, D.C.: GPO, 1998).

14. E. D. Cooke, "The Role of ALA and Other Library Associations in the Promotion of Library Legislation," in *Federal Aid to Libraries: Its History, Impact, Future,* ed. G. M. Casey, *Library Trends* 24 (July 1975); Redmond Kathleen Molz, *The Federal Roles in Support of Public Library Services: An Overview* (Chicago: American Library Association, 1990); Peggy Sullivan, *Carl H. Millam and the American Library Association* (New York: H. W. Wilson, 1976); Dennis Thomison, *A History of the American Library Association* (Chicago: American Library Association, 1978); and Wayne A. Wiegand and Dorothy Steffens, *Members of the Club: A Look at One Hundred ALA Presidents,* Occasional Papers, no. 182 (Champaign: University of Illinois, Graduate School of Library and Information Science, 1988).

15. American Library Association, *ALA Handbook of Organization, 1999–2000* (Chicago: American Library Association, 1999), 139–140.

9

Power Dies
the Moment
Action Ceases

In *New American Blues: A Journey through Poverty to Democracy,* Earl Shorris contends that only through action can people become involved citizens.[1] And it is only through action that librarians will become involved community builders. As community builders, librarians preserve the ideals of information equity, intellectual freedom, and lifelong learning and demonstrate proactive efforts to meet society's challenges of social, economic, and environmental change identified in the policies of the American Library Association. Power dies the moment action ceases.[2]

This book has described the many dimensions of community as it is characterized by government agencies, community development corporations, comprehensive community initiatives, policy institutes, and social services organizations. The changing economic and ethnic composition of the people of the United States presents a complex setting in which to strive to build community. Librarians must ensure that library services correspond to community visions. The work of librarians can be matched to the efforts of comprehensive community initiatives, and this work builds capacity, enforces resiliency, and creates a common place where all are welcome.

Librarians have demonstrated that they do build community, and examples have been provided of librarians who work with fragile readers, new arrivals, rural youth, distressed communities, and economic developers. Through a profession-wide commitment to overcoming economic barriers that prevent poor people from electronic access, librarians have demonstrated that they can organize to address complete transformation of work life when our communities have changing needs.

Librarians are faced with a new set of complexities as the call to build community requires yet another reconfiguration of work along with the accompanying need for administrative support and implementation of new policies. The obligation to build community comes from many directions. It is important to remember that the most traditional of librarianship's activities—providing books to readers—continues to be essential to building community. In *An Empire Wilderness: Travels into America's Future*, Robert D. Kaplan describes the advice a counselor in the crime-ridden south side of Tucson gives poor children in a Second Chance classroom:

> I told them they do not need money to travel beyond these poor neighborhoods, just a library card.[3]

People continue to hold great faith in the libraries that librarians built even before the advent of computers. Very poor people still find magic in a book they may take home. This is our philosopher's stone.

Libraries as common space are viewed by planners as potential catalysts for community revitalization and as important to neighborhoods.[4] The Eugene (Oregon) Urban Design Charette is a recent encouraging example. The library's motto, Building for Generations, imprinted on Director Carol Hildebrand's business card, was established through a realization that the library could create good civic space through focus on urban planning issues.[5]

We have the book—emblematic of knowledge and the solving of mysteries. The book is a metaphor for the many forms that knowledge may take—journals, CDs, electronically transmitted Web images. We have the community space—the place where all are welcome. The assimilation of technology into the library is ongoing in terms of newer, more powerful electronics, but the ideological assimilation has been accomplished. We have incorporated the use of technology in service of traditional values.

The next shift needed is for librarianship to make formal recognition of and commitment of resources to the importance of community building. This recognition and commitment are imperative if the future is to include a role for the manifestation of the core values of librarianship.

To continue the work librarians have done to preserve the heritage of the past,

To sustain the work librarians have done to defend intellectual freedom,

To protect the work librarians have done to ensure information equity regardless of format, and

To activate the work librarians have done to provide opportunities for lifelong learning to the people they serve . . .

Librarianship must dedicate time, resources, and commitment at the policy level to guarantee that community building is a high priority for the profession and so that the nation's community builders include librarians as valued partners in every enterprise. Power dies the moment action ceases.

There must be a librarian at every table.

ENDNOTES

1. Earl Shorris, *New American Blues: A Journey through Poverty to Democracy* (New York: W. W. Norton, 1997), 254.

2. Ibid.

3. Robert D. Kaplan, *An Empire Wilderness: Travels into America's Future* (New York: Random House, 1998), 161.

4. William Fulton and Chris Jackson, "Let's Meet at the Library," *Planning* (May 1999): 4–9.

5. Southwestern Oregon AIA, *Eugene Urban Design Charette: Fitting the Library into Downtown* (Eugene, Ore.: AIA/SWO, January 1999).

INDEX

111

Kathleen de la Peña McCook is a professor at the University of South Florida, School of Library and Information Science, Tampa, where she is also coordinator for Community Outreach in the College of Arts and Sciences. She is a member of the Rural Social Services Partnership—a comprehensive community initiative, the Good Community Collaborative for Hillsborough County, REFORMA, the American Library Association, and the Florida Library Association. She is a contributing editor to *American Libraries* and was guest editor for the May 2000 issue on poverty, and editor of the summer 2000 *Library Trends* on "Diversity in Libraries." She has written and edited books and articles and has also been on the faculties at Louisiana State University, School of Library and Information Science, and the University of Illinois, Graduate School of Library and Information Science. She received a Ph.D. from the University of Wisconsin, School of Library and Information Studies, and her M.A. from the University of Chicago, Graduate Library School.